ARIZONA
Territory
Cook Book

Recipes from 1864 to 1912

by

Daphne Overstreet

GOLDEN WEST ☼ PUBLISHERS

Front Cover Photo: "The Chuck Wagon" courtesy of Special Collections, University of Arizona.

Back Cover Photos: Courtesy of Arizona Historical Society and Maricopa Community College Southwest Studies Program.

Interior photo/art credits:

Martha Summerhayes photo, page 7, courtesy Southwest Studies.

Pete Kitchen photo, page 39, courtesy of Special Collections, University of Arizona.

Cactus cartoons pages 9, 17 and 30 from *Cactus Country,* by Jim Willoughby, also published by Golden West Publishers.

Photo page 71—Stella Hughes, from the cover of *Bacon and Beans* ($12.95 + $1.75 s/h) by Stella Hughes, P.O. Box 1118 Eagle Creek, Clifton, Arizona 85533.

Note from the editor: In this book, the Tohono O'odham Indians are referred to as Papago, a term used in territorial times.

Library of Congress Cataloging-in-Publication Data

Overstreet, Daphne, 1951—
Arizona Territory Cook Book / by Daphne Overstreet
     p.   cm.
Includes index.
1. Cookery, American—Southwestern Style   2. Cookery, American-Southwestern style-History. 3. Cookery—Arizona.   4. Cookery-Arizona-History.   I. Title

TX715.2.S69084	1995	96-37279
641.59791—dc21		CIP

2nd Printing © 2004

Printed in the United States of America from material originally published by Pimeria Press, copyright © 1975 by Daphne Overstreet.

Golden West Publishers, Inc.
4113 N. Longview Ave.
Phoenix, AZ 85014, USA
(800) 658-5830

For free sample recipes and complete Table of Contents for every Golden West cookbook, visit our website: **goldenwestpublishers.com**

Table of Contents

Historical Profiles

Preface

Arizona's pioneer cookery is the aroma of salt pork and beans simmering over a prospector's open fire, the clatter of tin plates as hungry cowboys devour son-of-a-gun stew, and steaming tamales at a Mexican fiesta. It is also Indian women grinding corn into meal on stone metates, caldrons of soup in a company's mess tent, and Mormon pioneers preparing the fruits of their fields.

All the recipes in this book are from territorial days, 1864 to 1912, and reflect the lifestyles of those who called Arizona their home. The Indian, Mexican, military man, miner, cowboy, and Mormon left their prints not only on the land but in the cooking pot as well. This book is an attempt to place Arizona's distinctive cookery in historical perspective, to capture the memories of savory dishes before they fade away.

Cooking was more creative then than now. Ingredients were not always measured in cupfuls or tablespoons but by personal preferences and tastes. Many of the recipes given here were submitted without exact proportions, and rather than ruin the spirit of pioneer cooking, I leave it to you to discover the amounts for yourself.

Many pioneer families throughout the state deserve special thanks for so generously contributing their recipes. I am also indebted to Stella Hughes of Eagle Creek, Melba McNeil of the LDS Region Genealogical Library in Tucson, Phyllis Ball of Special Collections at the University of Arizona Library, and Lori Davisson and Winifred Smiley of the Arizona Historical Society. The staffs of the Arizona State Museum, Fort Verde Historical Museum, Navajo Tribal Museum, and Sharlot Hall Museum are also acknowledged for their help. To all a special thanks.

Daphne Overstreet

Photo courtesy of Arizona Historical Society

"Sometimes I hear the still voices of the desert. They seem to be calling me through the echoes of the past."

—*Martha Summerhayes*

Historical Profile

Martha Summerhayes

(1846-1911)

No doubt countless men and women have taken courage from this refined New England woman's account of life in the "dreaded and then unknown land" as she followed her beloved Lieutenant to the Arizona of the 1870s. "I had cast my lot with a soldier, and where he was, was home to me" she wrote in her classic Vanished Arizona.

Martha Dunham Summerhayes was born on Nantucket Island October 21, 1846. She was well educated and from a Puritan family who sent her abroad to study. During this time she became enamored with what appeared to be the glamour and intellectual stimulation of military life.

When she returned to Nantucket she was so warmly welcomed by "my old friend Jack" that the couple wed in March of 1874.

Within a few months, Jack's regiment, the 8th U.S. Infantry, was ordered to Arizona, that land of "perennial natural inconveniences from rattlesnakes to cactus thorns," all of which made it particularly miserable for a married man and his new bride.

Martha was so busy surviving the vicissitudes of frontier life that she did not write her recollections until 1908 when she and Jack returned to Nantucket to retire.

"We were no longer expecting sudden orders, and I was able to think quietly over the events of the past. My thoughts turned back to the days when we were all Lieutenants together marching across the deserts and mountains of Arizona...back to the days at Camp McDowell where we slept under the stars, swam in the red waters of the Verde River, ate canned peaches, pink butter and commissary hams, listened for the scratching of the centipedes as they

scampered around the edges of our canvas-covered floors, found scorpions in our slippers and rattlesnakes under our beds."

Though her experiences were unusually rough, the passing years softened the memories. Sensitive images emerged of the hated place. Her humor, compassion, curiosity and deep love of life transformed her personal experiences into a tale of courage for all time, which explains why the book has been often reprinted since her death in 1911.

Who would not succumb to this account of her journey up the Colorado River in the mid 1870s to Fort Mojave on the steamer "Gila":

"We had staterooms, but could not remain in them long at a time due to the intense heat. I had never felt such heat, and no one else ever had or has since. We wandered around the boat, first forward, then aft to find a cool spot. There was no ice, and consequently no fresh provisions. A Chinese man served as steward and cook, and at the ringing of a bell we all went into a small salon back of the pilothouse where the meals were served. Our party at table on the 'Gila' consisted of several officers with their wives, about eight or nine in all, and we could have had a merry time enough but for the awful heat, which destroyed both our good looks and our tempers. The fare was meagre, of course: fresh biscuits without butter, very salty boiled beef, and some canned vegetables, which were poor enough in those days. Pies made from preserved peaches or plums generally followed this course. Chinese cooks, as we all know, can make pies under conditions that would stagger most chefs. They may have no marble pastry slab, and the lard may run like oil, still they can make pies that taste good to the hungry traveler.

"But the dining room was hot! The metal handles of the knives were uncomfortably warm to the touch, and even the wooden arms of the chairs felt as if they were slowly igniting. After a hasty meal and a few remarks upon the salt beef and the general misery of our lot, we would seek some spot which might be a trifle cooler."

Martha Summerhayes died in 1911 two months after her beloved husband Jack. The two are buried together at Arlington National Cemetery.

Indians

Arizona's native inhabitants had been serving up tasty dishes for centuries before the territory was established. Considering the sparse vegetation and nearly nonexistent rainfall, surviving in the rough deserts and mountains was sheer wizardry. All in all, everyone ate simply but well. The desert yielded surprising amounts of wild edibles, game abounded, and small gardens produced limited amounts of corn, beans, squash and chiles, at least *most* of the time.

The importance of wild foods in the Indian diet cannot be underestimated. In a region where agriculture was difficult and crop yields uncertain, survival often depended on knowledge of desert plants.

The agave, or century plant, has always been especially important to the **Apaches,** though the delicacy was also enjoyed by **Hopis, Havasupais, Yavapais, Pimas,** and **Papagos.** Agave gathering was a social event for the Apache women. They would pry up the plants with long pointed poles, and then chop away the heavy leaves until only the heart of the plant remained. After two or three dozen were collected, they were baked for two days in a rock-lined pit covered with bear grass and earth. The sweet-tasting heart was eaten fresh from the pit, or dried and ground into meal for future use as gruel.

Other desert plants were, and still are, important in the Indian diet. Cholla buds and prickly pears were collected and prepared in a variety of ways, and the fruit of the saguaro was used for making syrup and ceremonial wine. Mesquite beans were more important than corn to the **Yumas, Mohaves,** and Papagos, who ground the beans into flour for bread and mush. Every part of the yucca was useful. The **Navajos** munched its stalk, the Hopis made soap from its roots, and several tribes boiled the flowers and ate them with seasoning.

With fall and early winter came piñon nut and acorn gathering time. Piñons have been a favorite of the Navajos and Havasupais for centuries, and the **Apaches** consider piñon mush excellent food for babies. The Havasupais would roast the nuts by shaking them with live coals in a basket. Then the nuts were shelled, ground, and made into cakes or boiled as gruel. Ground acorns were used mainly for thickening stews by the Apaches, Navajos, Pimas, Papagos, and Yavapais.

Besides collecting wild foods, the Indians hunted and fished. The Mohaves ate fish and beaver from the Colorado River. The Apaches' homeland provided them with wild turkey, quail, and deer. Rabbit was the main meat of the Hopis, though they also hunted antelope, wildcat, badger, porcupine, and desert rodents.

Finally there was agriculture. Before the Spaniards arrived in the 16th century, the only crops grown by Arizona Indians were corn, beans, and squash. The foreigners brought strange ideas and technology, which many of the Indians resisted, but new plants such as chile, wheat, melons, peaches, and apricots were adopted with enthusiasm.

Besides the wondrous new foods, the Spaniards also brought horses, sheep, goats, and cattle into the Southwest. The livestock especially affected the Navajos, who never had taken well to agriculture. These semi-nomadic people began pasturing sheep and goats, though they also maintained small cornfields and peach orchards. Mutton became the main food in their diet, and all edible parts were carefully used.

Corn has always been the most important cultivated crop, especially to the Hopis, who believe the first corn was given to mankind by supernatural beings. Special ceremonies still occur at corn-planting time, and there are numerous rites and songs to make corn grow. Besides its religious function, corn was also an important part of Hopi courtship and marriage customs. A Hopi maiden would make two small cakes of blue cornmeal and meat and tie them in white corn husks. After the cakes were fastened together, she would give them to her favorite suitor as a token of affection during Bean Dance time in February. It was also customary for the Hopi girl to propose by leaving blue corn piki bread on the young man's doorstep. If the bread was taken in, the proposal was accepted and wedding preparations soon began. Beans have also been a favorite Indian food since the ancient ancestors domesticated wild plants they found growing in canyons. Those first beans, called teparies, resisted insects and grew well with very little water. Teparies and pinto beans are cooked much the same today as in territorial times—boiled, refried or simmered with meat.

Though the menus and recipes in those early days were uncomplicated and lacked variety, the foods were healthful and nutritious. The Indians lived close to the land, and from its seeming barrenness they wrested berries, and roots, and garden crops where scarcely a drop of rain would fall. Food gathering, survival in its most immediate sense, occupied long hours, and what time was not spent combing the rugged land was spent in grinding corn and mesquite beans on the stone metate.

The recipes in this chapter represent the traditional foods and cooking methods employed by Arizona's first cooks during the territorial period. The recipes themselves are old as the ancestors and modern as today.

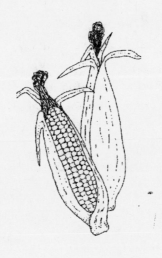

Hopi girls grinding corn, 1908

"Where, I wonder, shall we Rains go?

Where, I wonder, will they go, the Yellow Dragonfly
Boys, the Blue Dragonfly Maids?

Excellent growing corn! These Yellow-corn Maids—

Clouds perhaps will appear up yonder.

Here, here, the Rain will stand. Here, here, the
Rain will stand.

From each of the four directions Rain will come
side by side."

— *Hopi Corn Grinding Song*

Navajo Kneel Down Bread

Shuck fresh corn and scrape the kernels from the cobs. Then grind (on a metate) until corn is mushlike. Add a little salt. Mold mixture into oblong cakes 3 inches long and 2 inches wide. These should be about 1 inch thick. Meanwhile, soak corn husks in hot water until soft. Then wrap the cakes in the husks with narrow ends turned under. The way the bread is wrapped suggests a person kneeling, hence its name.

Dig a pit about 9 inches deep and 2 feet square. Build a fire and rake out the coals when the pit is thoroughly hot. Next, pile the cakes in the pit and place some wet corn husks over all. Now cover the pit with hot ashes and dirt, and build a small fire on top. Bake slowly, preferably overnight.

Yuma Squash

Peel squash, cut into chunks, and boil until tender. When squash is well cooked, drain off liquid and mash. Then stir squash that has been salted into melted lard for flavoring.

Navajo Blue Bread

**2 cups finely ground blue cornmeal (white or
   yellow can be substituted)**
2 tablespoons juniper ashes
1 cup boiling water
pinch salt

Place juniper ashes in a bowl and add boiling
water. Stir mixture well and then strain. Now add
water to cornmeal to make dough. Roll about 2
tablespoons of dough into a ball and flatten into a
cake. Bake on greased griddle 10 minutes on each
side.

*Navajo
Sand
Painting*

Navajo Corn Griddle
Cakes

Mix 4 cups of corn flour with 2 teaspoons baking
powder and enough water or goat's milk to make a
thick batter. Pull off hunks of the dough and pat into
thin cakes about 6 inches in diameter. Cook on a
greased griddle about 3 minutes on each side.

Pima & Papago Squash Blossoms

Pick a dozen squash blossoms and simmer in small amount of water until tender. Drain well and mash. Meanwhile, cut fresh corn from cob and simmer 1/2 hour in just enough water to cover. Then add the squash blossoms to corn and continue cooking until mixture thickens. Add salt.

Pima Basket Design

Apache Fry Bread

4 heaping handfuls of flour
1/4 handful of baking powder
very little salt

Mix flour, baking powder, and salt with water to a consistency of bread dough. Batter must not be sticky, but must be dry enough to knead. Shape into balls about 2 inches across. Flatten into an 8-inch circle by patting with hands. Cook in 3/4-inch-deep grease that is very hot and just about smoking. Turn one time. Drain on absorbent paper. The bread will swell up and have large bubbles. Do not cook to crispness.

Pumpkin

Pumpkins have been cultivated by Arizona Indians for centuries and are still an important crop.

Pima, Papago, and Havasupai: Cut a peeled pumpkin into small pieces. Now shell fresh corn from 3 cobs and mash to pulp. Mix corn and pumpkin together and cook in about 1 cup of water until pumpkin is soft. Add salt and serve hot.

Apache: Simmer cubed pumpkin until tender, and mash. Add 2 to 3 tablespoons ground sunflower seeds to each cup of pumpkin. Season lightly with salt.

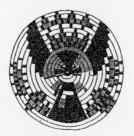

Hopi Tray

Hopi Sprouts

Simmer a container of bean sprouts for about 2 hours. Shell several ears of dried corn and boil separately. Fry some salt pork. Add the pork, drippings, and corn to the boiled sprouts. Cook all together in some of the corn liquid for about an hour.

Beans

Beans have been an important staple of Arizona's Indians since aboriginal times. Refried beans were prepared in much the same manner by all the groups.

Soak pinto beans overnight in cold water. Next day add more water and salt, and simmer slowly until beans are tender. A piece of salt pork or fatty bacon can be added for flavor. To refry beans, mash the cooked beans to make a paste. Then fry in lard. This is eaten spread on fry bread or tortillas.

Cholla Buds

Carefully pick the buds off the cholla cactus. The Indians cleaned the thorns off by shaking small pieces of sandstone with the buds in a basket. Another way is to boil the buds for about 1/2 hour, drain, and rinse well. Pull off any thorns that did not fall off during cooking. Add fresh water to cover, and simmer until tender.

Hopi: Simmer buds for 2 hours in water with whole ears of sweet corn for flavoring.

Pima and Papago: Chop one onion, 2 seeded chiles, and about 24 cholla buds. Fry in lard with 1/2 pound thinly sliced meat. Cook until meat is tender. Add salt to taste.

Hopi Prickly Pear

Pick tender prickly pear pads in the spring.

To cook, put the pads in a big pot with lots of water. Add several ears of sweet corn for flavor. Cook 4 hours and then scrape off thorns with a sharp knife. Serve prickly pear in its own liquid after liquid has been strained to remove thorns.

The **Pimas** and **Papagos** ate prickly pear boiled alone until tender, or sliced fine and fried in grease.

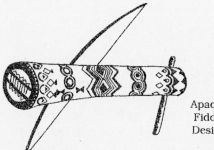

Apache
Fiddle
Design

Apache Acorn Stew

2 pounds beef
1 cup ground acorns
salt

Cut beef into chunks and simmer until tender. When meat is done, separate the stock. Add acorn meal to meat and mix well. Now pour stock over mixture, stir well and serve.

Hopi Corn Stew

2 cups green corn shelled from cob
1 cup finely chopped beef or goat
1 cup chopped squash
1 tablespoon flour
salt

Fry meat in lard until brown. Add remaining ingredients and water to cover. When squash is nearly cooked, stir in flour that has been made into a paste with a little water. Stir well, and cook 5 minutes more.

Papago
Basket
Design

Papago Corn & Pumpkin Stew

3 ears corn
1 unripe (green) pumpkin
1 cup water
salt to taste

Peel and seed pumpkin and cut into small pieces. Shell corn from the cob and mash into a pulp. Combine, add water and simmer until pumpkin is soft. Serve while hot.

Navajo Mutton Stew

Cut mutton into small pieces and place in boiling water. Add onions and potatoes, and cook until done. Salt last.

*Navajo
Sand
Painting*

Navajo Piñon Nuts

Roast piñon nuts in a frying pan until they crack. Grind to break shells and then winnow in a pan. The nuts can be ground up and molded into small cakes, or mixed with roasted corn.

*Navajo
Sand
Painting*

Navajo Jack Rabbit Stew

Dress the rabbit and boil with corn flour and salt. The rabbit may be fried if preferred.

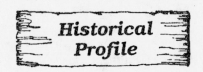

Captain
John G. Bourke

(1843-1896)

Captain John Bourke earned a reputation as an ethnologist, folklorist, and military chronicler as well as respect for his deeds as a combat officer. He served for many years on the staff of General George Crook, the famous Indian fighter. The two first met in 1871 and immediately felt an empathy since both were avid supporters of Indian rights. Both Bourke and Crook shared a great respect for the Apaches who they fought in Arizona, and Bourke supported Crook's unorthodox methods of ending hostilities. The pair saw the Indian leaders, Geronimo, Loco, Nana, Bonito, Chihuahua, Chato, Ulzana, Mangus, Zele, and Kayatennae as "men of noticeable brain power, physically perfect, and mentally acute—just the individuals to lead a forlorn hope in the face of every obstacle."

In his writings, Bourke records details not only of Indian campaigns, but carries on a strong defense of the Apache people and criticizes the government's inadequate Indian policy to deal with their well being. Bourke and Crook passionately believed the Apaches should become self-supporting and govern themselves on their reservation. Bourke was recording details of Apache life with fairness and openmindedness at a time when territory newspapers, such as the Tombstone Epitaph, were describing them as fiends and suggesting ways readers might murder peaceful Apaches and get away with it.

Though Bourke's first writings were motivated by his desire to support Crook's efforts on behalf of the Apaches and debunk negative rumors Crook's enemies were circulating, his popularity was growing among audiences eager for news about military life and other western topics. He had the ability to transport his readers into the dusty terrain and introduce them to colorful living characters. Fortunately, he was as interested in the cooking pot as he was in details of the campaigns.

We know, for instance, that during the famous 1883 campaign when Crook (accompanied by Bourke) chased the Apaches into the Sierra Madre, the Indians were dining rather sumptuously in spite of being on the run. In An Apache Campaign in the Sierra Madre, first published in 1886, Bourke describes hearing rifle shots in the distance as the troops trailed the Indians far behind. "Twenty carcasses demonstrated that they were not the worst of shots; neither were they, by any means, the worst of cooks," he reported. When the command finally reached the Apache encampment they found quickly-constructed shelter of branches and grass or stones and boards covered with gunny sacks. Nearby "smoke curled gracefully towards the sky from crackling embers, in front of which, transfixed on wooden spits, were the heads, hearts and livers of the afternoon's catch. Another addition was a cotton-tailed rabbit run down by these fleet-footed Bedouins of the Southwest. Meanwhile a couple of scouts were making bread—the light, thin tortilla of the Mexicans, baked quickly and not bad eating," he remarked.

He went on to note that the Apaches could find food ("and pretty good food, too") where a Caucasian would starve. His epic catalog of desert edibles included cactus seeds, wild acorns, mesquite gum and numerous desert creatures that all stave off the pangs of hunger and "represent merely a few of the resources" of an Apache on his own. Contrast this abundant native diet with the rations of the cavalry on this same campaign: "The rations consisted of hard-bread, coffee and bacon for 60 days, and all was carried on pack mules," Bourke reported. And finally, there is this gem from Bourke's diary entry of May 2, 1883 as the Crook expedition crossed the border into Mexico in pursuit of the Apaches:

"Martin, the cook, deserves some notice. He was not, as he himself admitted, a French cook by profession. His early life had been passed in the more romantic occupation of driving an ore wagon between Willcox and Globe, and to quote his own boast, he could 'hold down a sixteen-mule team with any outfit this side of the Rio Grande.' "But what he lacked in culinary knowledge he more than made up in strength and agility. He was not less than six feet two in his socks, and built like a young Hercules. He was gentle-natured too, and averse to fighting. Such, as least, was the opinion I gathered from a remark he made the first evening I was thrown into his society.

"His eyes somehow were fixed on mine, while he said quietly, 'If there's anybody here don't like the grub, I'll kick a lung out of him!' I was just about to suggest that a couple of pounds less saleratus in the bread and a couple of gallons less water in the coffee would be grateful to my Sybarite palate; but after this conversation, I reflected that the fewer the remarks I made the better would be the chances of my enjoying the rest of the trip, so I said nothing. Martin, I believe, is now in Chihuahua, and I assert from the depths of an outraged stomach, that a better man or a worse cook never thumped a mule or turned a flapjack."

In addition to the book just quoted, Bourke wrote The Snake Dance of the Moquis in 1884, General Crook in Indian Country, and his monumental classic, On the Border with Crook, in 1891. All of his works have been reprinted and are available to those who appreciate a candid look at the Arizona of those days.

Mexicans

The cultural influences of Spaniards and Mexicans were indelibly printed on Arizona long before territorial times. Father Kino had established missions and ranches by 1700, and soon after came the development of haciendas, silver mines, and presidios. But the Apaches ended any promise of peace, and by the 1840s the harassed Mexicans were forced to abandon the mines and their homes. Before the United States purchased southern Arizona from Mexico in 1854, the few hundred remaining Mexicans had already sought protection behind Tucson's presidio walls.

Conditions on the frontier improved after troops, which had been withdrawn during the Civil War, moved into the territory to protect the settlers. By the '70s and '80s many Mexicans were migrating back to work in Arizona's mines and on the railroad.

Mexican clothing, architecture, and cooking were perfectly adapted to the southern Arizona environment, and though hordes of Anglos were pouring in from every direction, Mexican customs held on and helped create the distinctive character of the territory.

During her stay at Ehrenberg in 1875, Martha Summerhayes, an army wife, noted the cooking methods and clothing of the Mexican women. How she envied their simple, airy kitchens and loose fitting blouses! The frijoles bubbling over the open fire and tortillas baking on hot sheet iron made the cumbersome equipment in her own army kitchen seem unbearable by comparison.

How wistfully she must have watched the Mexican ladies during that searing summer. She wrote, "The women were scrupulously clean and always wore a low-necked and short-sleeved white linen blouse. Over this they wore a calico skirt. When they ventured out, the younger women put on muslin gowns and carried parasols. Oh! If only I could dress as the Mexicans do. Their necks and arms do look so cool and clean."

In spite of this outburst she continued to swelter in high-necked, long-sleeved white dresses. "We kept up the table in American fashion and ate American food in so far as we could get it. How I wished I had no silver, no table linen, no china and could adopt the customs of my neighbors."

Even before Martha Summerhayes arrived in Arizona, the hospitality of the Pete Kitchen Ranch near Nogales and the culinary talents of Pete's wife, Doña Rosa, were famous from Tucson to Hermosillo. Doña Rosa loved to cook for the desert travelers who would pass their way. It was a perfect excuse for some choice dish or perhaps a fiesta. Captain John Bourke wrote, "If food were not already on the fire, some of the women set about the preparation of the savory and spicy stews for which the Mexicans are deservedly famous, and others kneaded the dough and patted into shape the paper-thin tortillas with which to eat the juicy frijoles or dip up the tempting chili Colorado."

When southern Arizona became too civilized for the Kitchens during the 1880s, they decided to sell their ranch. Doña Rosa gave a farewell party that would never be forgotten. The day was set and word spread like fire. Doña Rosa expected guests from all over the Santa Cruz Valley, from Tucson, Tubac, Calabasas, and Nogales. It took three days to prepare the food, and Doña Rosa, needless to say, was in her element.

Mountains of tortillas were made, turkeys, hogs, and chickens were roasted, and dozens of small cakes with colored icing were lovingly prepared. When the big day arrived, wagons and buckboards clogged the roadway. Everyone was going to the fiesta, to dance, to sing, and to sit by the outdoor bonfires and feast at the tables sagging with the weight of the food.

Mexican food today is the legacy of the Aztecs who were dining sumptuously on beans, corn, chiles, avocados, onions, and chocolate before Cortez arrived in the New World. The tortilla, for example, has not changed in 400 years. Masa has always been the Mexican staff of life. As in ancient times, it is prepared by soaking dry corn kernels in lime water until they are soft. The resulting hominy is then rinsed and ground into moist dough. In territorial times, the women kneeled over their stone grinding troughs, called metates, and crushed the corn with a stone called a mano. Masa is the basic ingredient for tortillas and tamales. Fresh masa can be purchased at local tortilla factories throughout the Southwest, and dry packaged masa is available at some markets.

The pioneer recipes in this chapter are used in the same way today as in territorial times.

Making Tortillas   *Photo courtesy of Arizona Historical Society*

Flour Tortillas

Mix 2 cups flour, 1 teaspoon salt, 1 1/2 tea-spoons baking powder, and 1 tablespoon lard. Add enough cold water to make a stiff dough. Knead dough until smooth and elastic. Make small balls and pat out very thin. Cook on lightly greased griddle.

How I envied them the simplicity of their lives! Besides, the tortillas were delicious to eat, and as for the frijoles, they were beyond anything I had ever eaten in the shape of beans. I took lessons in the making of tortillas. A woman was paid to come and teach me; but I never mastered the art. It is in the blood of the Mexican, and a girl begins at a very early age to make the tortilla. It is the most graceful thing to see a pretty Mexican toss the wafer-like disc over her bare arms, and pat it out until transparent.

This was their supper; for, like nearly all people in the tropics, they ate only twice a day. Their fare was varied sometimes by a little carni seca, pounded up and stewed with chili verde or chile colorado.

— Martha Summerhayes, 1875

Corn Tortillas

Mix 2 cups corn meal or masa with 1 teaspoon salt. Add enough warm water to make a stiff dough. Let dough sit for 20 minutes. Then wet hands and roll dough into balls the size of hens' eggs. Pat into thin rounds and cook on slightly greased griddle.

Now if you could hear the soft, exquisite, affectionate drawl with which the Mexican woman says chili verde you could perhaps come to realize what an important part the delicious green pepper plays in the cookery of these countries. They do not use it in its raw state, but generally roast it whole, stripping off the thin skin and throwing away the seeds, leaving only the pulp, which acquires a fine flavor by having been roasted or toasted over the hot coals.
— Martha Summerhayes, 1875

Chile Kellanada

Take green chile peppers, roast, peel, and cut off tops. After seeds are removed, fill the chiles with a mixture of grated Mexican cheese, chopped olives, and chopped onions. Dip stuffed chiles in egg and cracker meal, and fry in hot lard. Serve immediately.

Frijoles

Wash 2 cups of pinto beans and put into a heavy pot filled with water. Bring to a boil, cover, and simmer slowly until beans are tender. If more liquid is needed, add a little boiling water. Cold water will darken the beans. Add salt after beans have been cooking about an hour.

When beans are tender, drain, and save the broth. Mash beans, add 3 tablespoons hot lard, and mix well. Return some of the broth to the beans until the consistency is like thick mush. Beans can be refried in hot lard before serving.

Chiles

Toast fresh green chile pods over flame until skin blisters. Put pods on a cloth, sprinkle with water, and cover with another cloth to steam a few minutes. The skins will peel off easily. Slit the skinned chiles and remove the seeds, which are the hottest part.

After peeling, chiles can be chopped or mashed

Mexican Cheese

Pour 10 gallons of milk into large crock or porcelain container and allow to become room temperature. Then add 2 dissolved rennet tablets, and stir thoroughly with hand. The milk will become curds and whey, with the curds settling at the bottom. Remove as much whey as possible with a cup. When curds become like cottage cheese, place in a large frying pan and add salt to taste. Cook over low heat, and stir constantly with a wooden spatula. If curds drain whey while cooking, pour off immediately. When cheese is cooked, it will become one large stringy ball. Turn off heat, and cut cheese into pieces the size of a biscuit. Flatten cheese by patting with hands into a small tortilla shape, and then fold in half. This recipe makes from 12 to 18 cheeses.

— *Eloisa Ferrer de Leon*

Calabacitas
(Squash)

Cut 6 summer or zucchini squash into small pieces. Fry 1 chopped onion, 2 chopped tomatoes, and green pepper in lard. Add the squash and cook slowly until soft. Then add about 1/2 cup milk and 1/2 pound crumbled cheese. Mash all ingredients together. Salt and pepper to taste.

— *Victoria Martinez*

Elotes

Select ripe, tender ears of corn fresh from the field. Pull husks down and strip off silks. Replace husks and put corn on hot coals to roast. Cook until tender, turning several times. Cooking time is usually 20 to 30 minutes.

Nopalitos

Collect small tender prickly pear pads and scrape off the thorns. Cut into chunks and simmer until tender. Drain and rinse. In another pan, heat about 1/2 cup grease and saute onions, green chile, and chopped tomatoes. Add a little flour and water to make a gravy. Add the prickly pears and cook about 15 minutes.

— *Victoria Martinez*

Puchero

(Mexican Soup)

Boil dry garbanzo beans, garlic, and onion with a good soup bone. Skim off liquid until it is clear. When garbanzos are nearly cooked, add squash blossoms, fresh corn cut from cob, and cubed squash. Simmer until vegetables are tender.

— *Aida Gonzales*

Bean Soup

1 pint frijoles (pintos)
2 quarts cold water
1 sliced onion
2 cloves garlic
1 chile pulp or 1 1/2 teaspoons chili powder
1/2 tablespoon salt
1 tablespoon oregano

Wash frijoles well and soak overnight. Boil very slowly. When frijoles are half done, add salt. When tender, add onion, chili, and garlic. Simmer until all are tender. Rub through a colander and reheat. Add water until soup is consistency of a purée.

Sopa De Queso

(Cheese Soup)

1 pound Mexican cheese, crumbled
5 medium potatoes
6 green chiles, roasted, peeled, and seeded
1/2 cup fresh milk
10 cups boiling water
2 tablespoons shortening, for frying potatoes

Peel, slice, and fry potatoes. Place potatoes in cooking pot and add cheese, chiles, boiling water, and milk. Salt to taste. Bring to boil and simmer for 20 minutes. Serves six.

— *Lucy DeSenz*

Albondigas

(Meatball Soup)

Mix 1 1/4 pounds of lean beef with 1 egg, 2 tablespoons flour, chopped white onion, cilantro (chopped fresh coriander leaves), a little white rice, and a few leaves of mint. Roll into small balls the size of a walnut.

In a large pot melt 2 tablespoons of grease or lard. When hot, add more chopped onion, diced green chile, several ripe tomatoes cut small, and salt and pepper. Add about a quart of water and bring to a boil. Drop the meatballs into the liquid and simmer over a slow fire until well done, about 1 hour.

— *Victoria Martinez*

Cazuela
(Stewed Jerky)

2 pounds beef jerky
1 teaspoon flour
1 cup chopped fresh tomatoes
1/2 cup chopped green chiles
8 cups water
1/4 cup chopped green onions
1/3 cup chopped cilantro
1 clove garlic
1 teaspoon oregano
2 medium potatoes
2 teaspoons lard
salt to taste

Soak jerky in water for 15 minutes. Pound jerky to separate fiber and to fluff the meat. Peel and dice potatoes in 1-inch cubes. Fry onions, chile, tomatoes, and cilantro slowly in lard. Add beef, garlic, oregano, and flour. Add water and salt. Bring to a boil and simmer about 20 minutes. Serves 6 to 8.

All Mexican housewives have two stones to pound the jerky. Usually these are selected from stream beds. Both must be smooth. One is round or oval and about fist size for pounding. The other is larger and heavier with a flat top on which to place the jerky to be pounded.

— *Lucy DeSenz*

Pozole

Soak dried maize kernels in lime water to hull the corn. Then wash corn in fresh water. Add cooked pork loin, beef, or game that has been cut into small pieces. Next add cooked pinto beans and green chile peppers that have been roasted and peeled. Be sure to remove the seeds. Garlic cloves and onions are added last. Mix all ingredients together and bring to a boil.

This stew is a traditional Arizona-Sonora recipe adapted from the Aztecan dish consisting of meats, cereals, and vegetables with seasoning.

— *Alberto Pradeau*

Bollos

To each cup of flour, add 1 teaspoon baking powder and a dash of salt. Add enough water to make a stiff dough and roll out flat. Cut dough into triangles, squares, and circles about 4 or 5 inches wide. Fry in deep fat until bollos puff up and turn brown. Cut open and fill with preserves or honey.

— *Aida Gonzales*

Chile Con Carne

(Chile with Meat)

2 pounds beef
4 cloves chopped garlic
2 tablespoons lard or drippings
3 bay leaves
1 chopped onion
1 quart ripe tomatoes or 1 large can tomatoes
1 cup chile pulp
1 tablespoon oregano
1 tablespoon salt
1 pint ripe olives

Cut the meat into small cubes. Brown garlic and onion. Add meat and steam. Rub tomatoes through a colander and add to meat. Now stir in chile pulp and cook for 20 minutes. Next, add seasonings and cook for 2 hours. Add cut-up olives last and cook for additional 1/2 hour. Serve with frijoles and tortillas.

The spacious mansion of Don Solomon, and especially the very roomy kitchen, was full of women preparing all sorts of things for the coming fiesta of San Juan. Turkeys and chickens were slaughtered and plucked, red pepper was being ground upon two metates at once, dried maize leaves were soaked, stretched and dried to envelop the toothsome tamale; cornmeal cakes were patted flat and fried to assume the beautiful sprinkled appearance of enchiladas, while a professional baker busied himself in the manufacture of biscochuelos and other sweets.

— Frank C. Lockwood

Mexican Chocolate

2 squares grated chocolate
1/2 cup boiling water
2 cups milk and 1 cup cream
3 tablespoons sugar
1 teaspoon cinnamon
1 egg
pinch of salt
pinch of nutmeg
1 teaspoon vanilla

Boil chocolate in water for 5 minutes, as this brings out the flavor. Then add milk, cream, sugar, salt, egg, and spices. Cook in double boiler for 1 hour, beating vigorously about every 10 minutes. The chocolate should be frothy.

Mexican Rice

Put a cup of uncooked white rice in pan, and fry in lard with a teaspoon of salt. Add finely chopped onion, green chile, and diced tomato. Add water and simmer until dry.

Fruit or Pumpkin Empanadas

Crust:
- **5 cups flour**
- **1 cup lard**
- **1 teaspoon salt**
- **1 teaspoon baking powder**
- **3 tablespoons sugar**

Mix all ingredients and add enough water to make a stiff dough. Make small balls out of dough and roll out to the size of a pancake. Place filling in center and fold crust in half. Crimp edges to keep fruit or pumpkin from draining out. Place on cookie sheet and bake at 375 degrees for 30 minutes.

Fruit filling may be stewed apricots, prunes, apples or canned cherries and peaches. Add cloves, allspice, cinnamon, and sugar to fruit.

For pumpkin filling, add 1 cup brown sugar, a dash of cloves, nutmeg, cinnamon, and salt, to about 3 cups, cooked pumpkin. Cook 10 minutes, stirring constantly, and cool before making empanadas.

Piñon nuts, almonds or raisins may also be added to the fillings.

— *Livia Leon Montiel*

Capirotada

(Pudding made for Lenten Fridays)

1 loaf white bread
2 1/2 cups panocha (brown sugar)
1/2 pound grated cheese
3/4 cup butter
1 cup raisins
1 stick cinnamon
1 pinch cloves
3 small onions, chopped
1 tablespoon fresh cilantro (coriander leaves)
2 cups water

Fry onions in butter. Crush panocha and cinnamon and add to onions. Now add water and simmer until panocha is dissolved. This should make a syrup about the consistency of maple syrup. Add cilantro and cloves, and simmer another 5 minutes. Brown bread on both sides in oven, and then arrange a layer of toasted bread in a deep baking dish. Now add a layer of raisins and cheese. Make a second layer of bread, and repeat until dish is filled. Pour syrup mixture over all and bake in slow oven until firm, about 45 minutes. Serve hot.

— *Marie Larivee*

Pete Kitchen

(about 1820-1895)

Pete Kitchen had a 1,000-acre ranch just north of Nogales from 1854 to the early 1870s. This is a noteworthy statement because Apache raiders drove every other rancher from the area.

His hacienda (which is now a restaurant) resembled a flat-roofed fort where sentinels were stationed. In case of a raid, warning shots called the ranch hands and farm workers from the surrounding fields to the main house where rifles were passed out.

According to reports from noted Arizona historian, Frank Lockwood, even Doña Rosa, Pete's wife, would "tie up her skirts like trousers, seize a gun and give the Apaches a reception as hot as her Mexican dishes."

The Apaches shot Pete's pigs full of arrows, killed his herder and his stepson, but the stubborn rancher held on to his reputation as being "more terrible than any army with banners." In time the Apaches passed him by.

He was regarded as the connecting link between savagery and civilization during those early days, and his ranch was the safest outpost for travelers, settlers, and miners between Tucson and Magdalena, Sonora. His door was always open and his hospitality was legendary. From his abundant harvests he fed guests on wild turkey, smoked ham and bacon, choice melons, potatoes, cabbages and various fruits of the season.

His smoked hams were so prized in Tucson that stores would boast in tall lettered signs, "Pete Kitchen Hams." He supplied these delicacies to markets from Nogales to Silver City, New Mexico.

According to a report in the Tucson Citizen of June 15, 1872, he had 20 acres in potatoes at the time, had cured 14,000 pounds of bacon and ham, and had marketed 5,000 pounds of lard. The rancher's income from this vast production was no less than $10,000, a tidy sum at the time.

Kitchen was a lively and charismatic character. Everybody in the Santa Cruz Valley seemed to know him and look forward to his periodic trips to Tucson. He was so popular a group of men and boys would go out as far as San Xavier to meet the traveler with his ox-cart filled with hams and produce.

His image was colorful—steel gray eyes peering out from under the brim of a wide sombrero and a serape over his shoulder. Even his sayings were widely quoted, especially the one describing the road to Sonora which he traveled, "Tucson, Tubac, Tumacacori to Hell!"

Kitchen sold his ranch and moved to Tucson when the railroad came to Arizona since newly arriving foodstuffs cut markedly into his profits, but he continued to buy and sell cattle from Sonora.

Lockwood honored Kitchen by calling him "a man of no ordinary calibre. Apart from his force, resolution, and general likableness, he was a man of power and character, the ideal of the Border man of his day—brave, friendly, magnanimous, but also profane, a regular drinker, and a diligent knight of the green table." Lockwood went on to speculate that it was because he combined these good and bad qualities in frontier perfection that he was so famous and esteemed.

The Military

The United States acquired the territory that became Arizona as a result of the Mexican War of 1848 and the Gadsden Purchase of 1854. Military garrisons had been established to keep peace in the area and protect settlers from Indian attacks. At the start of the Civil War, however, the troops were withdrawn, and the Apaches, who saw the Anglos as trespassers on their land, were convinced they had driven the military away. Encouraged by this belief, they retaliated with new strength against the pale invaders who had come with picks and mules, cattle and wagon trains.

After the Civil War, regular companies of cavalry and infantry returned to the territory, and fort building continued for the next two decades.

The troops had their hands full from the start. Arizona was an isolated, thorny frontier. Maintaining headquarters and simply surviving required arduous labor.

Rough buildings of adobe or wood housed the men. Captain John Bourke wrote, "The houses were veritable museums of entomology with the choicest specimens of centipedes, scorpions and tarantulas." Bourke was referring to Camp Grant, but conditions varied little from post to post in the 1870s. He went on to say, "There was nothing else to do but scout after the Apaches who were very bold and kept the garrison occupied."

On the few rare occasions of peace and quiet, the men passed the time as they could. Some amused themselves by reading newspapers, usually weeks old, from San Francisco, New York, and other cities. Others invented diversions such as collecting and exhibiting rattlesnakes, tarantulas, and spiders in glass bottles, and those who found desert post life too tedious and unbearable drank and gambled their leisure hours away. Many would have hunted, but usually it was too dangerous to leave the garrison. Captain Camillus Carr wrote, "What land was not occupied by reptiles and cactus seemed to be well held down by the perniciously active Apache, and no one was allowed to go half a mile away from the post in broad daylight without a suitable escort."

Mealtime at the posts was an exercise in monotony. So much so, in fact, that it is consistently not mentioned by chroniclers of the time. Volumes have been written on the searing temperatures, rude buildings, and Apache attacks, but scarcely a word is written about the daily mess.

The official ration during territorial days consisted of pork or bacon, soft or hard bread, beans, coffee, tea, sugar, vinegar, salt, pepper, potatoes and molasses. Fresh vegetables, eggs, and dairy products were simply not included in the soldier's regimen.

There was one saving grace, however. To supplement their diets, the men could buy canned fruits and vegetables and other rarities from the Subsistence Department at their posts.

Almost everything was boiled. Stews and hash were the main staples, backed up by bread and beans. Cattle were kept at some of the posts, but the beef was usually as tough as old boot leather. The flour for bread wasn't much better. The gritty stuff was imported from Sonora, where soft stones were used to grind the grain. Fresh fruits and vegetables were nearly impossible to get in some places, but other posts had fairly successful gardens where melons, beans, corn, and greens were raised.

What little good food may have been available was often spoiled by the cooks. For the most part they were untrained novices unblessed with culinary skills and imagination. Enormous quantities of food were wasted owing to their blunders.

Scouting party rations in Arizona were even less delicious. An anonymous account of military life in 1869 describes the fare: "The ration usually carried on the mountain scouts consists of pork, flour, coffee, and sugar. The flour is eaten as flapjacks fried in pork fat. Very seldom are the men able to improve their diet by killing deer, antelope or turkey on account of the scarcity of time for hunting while engaged on these expeditions." The writer went on to explain that pinole, a mixture of cornmeal and water, and jerky were the only provisions carried on scouts when the smoke from cooking fires could reveal the soldiers' whereabouts to the Apaches.

Life was not always grim. Parties, balls, and dinners held at the posts were surprisingly lavish affairs, with fine china and linen supplied by the officers' wives.

Even in remote outposts, special occasions were observed with some flair in spite of the adverse conditions. Lieutenant John Bigelow, for example, while on a scouting expedition during Christmas of 1885, ended up at the Mowry Mine with his men for the holiday. Eager to make the best of a bad

Kitchen at Fort McDowell   *Photo courtesy of Sharlot Hall Museum*

situation, he scheduled races and other athletic events, and a roast pig for dinner. No one in camp had any experience in pit barbecuing except the packer, who dug a hole and buried the pork in embers, gunny sacks, and earth. Bigelow was delighted with the cooked results. "A piece presented to me for dinner was the most savory pork viand I have ever tasted," he wrote.

Finally there was the unusual situation. Camp Lowell, on the outskirts of Tucson, was always an important military post. The unmarried officers boarded in town and took many of their meals at the Shoo Fly Restaurant.

The Shoo Fly was named on the principle that "the flies won't shoo worth a cent, but like the poor, they are always with us."

Captain Bourke's colorful description of the place in 1869 is a priceless relic of territorial times:

"It was a long, narrow, low-ceiled room of adobe, whose walls were washed in a neutral yellowish tint, whose floor was of rammed earth and ceiling of white muslin. Place here and there eight or ten tables of different sizes; cover them with cheap cloths, cheap china and glass—I use the term "cheap" in regard to quality only, and not in regard to the price, which had been dear enough.

"Put one large, cheap mirror on the wall facing the main entrance, and not far from it a wooden clock, which probably served some mysterious purpose other than time-keeping, because it was never wound up. Have pine benches, and home-made chairs, with raw-hide bottoms fastened with strings of the same material to the framework. Make the place look decidedly neat and clean, notwithstanding the flies and the hot alkali dust which penetrated upon the slightest excuse. Bring in two bright, pleasant-mannered Mexican boys, whose dark complexions were well set off by neat white cotton jackets and loose white cotton trousers, with sometimes a colored sash about the waist. Give each of these young men a fly-flapper as a badge of office, and the 'Shoo Fly' is open for the reception of guests.

"Napkins designated the seats of the regular boarders. 'Mealers' were not entitled to such distinction and never seemed to expect it. There was no bill of fare. None was needed. Boarders always knew what they were going to get—same old thing. There never was any change during all the time of my acquaintance with the establishment which, after all is said and done, certainly contrived to secure for its patrons all that the limited market facilities of the day afforded. Beef was not always easy to procure, but there was no lack of bacon, chicken, mutton, and kid meat. Potatoes ranked as luxuries of the first class, and never sold for less than ten cents a pound, and often could not be had for love or money.

"There was plenty of 'jerked' beef, savory and palatable enough in stews and hashes; eggs, and the sweet, toothsome black 'frijoles' of Mexico; tomatoes equal to those of any part of our country, and lettuce always crispy, dainty, and delicious. For fresh fruit, our main reliance was upon the 'burro' trains coming up from the charming oasis of Hermosillo, the capital of Sonora—a veritable garden of the Hesperides, in which Nature was most lavish with her gifts of honey-juiced oranges, sweet limes, lemons, edible quinces, and luscious apricots; but the apple, the plum, and the cherry were unknown to us, and the strawberry only occasionally seen."

The recipes in this chapter were taken from U.S. Army sources of the territorial era, and represent the daily mess of Arizona's enlisted men.

Hardtack

- **4 cups flour**
- **4 teaspoons salt**
- **water**

Mix flour and salt together. Add just enough water to make a heavy dough that will not stick to the hands. Roll out the dough until it is 1/2 inch thick. Cut into pieces about 3 inches square and then punch 16 holes in each piece with a nail. Turn pieces over and punch through again. Bake on ungreased light metal sheet in oven about 375 degrees for half an hour. Tack should be light brown on both sides.

Hardtack is broken fairly easily when fresh, but as it dries out it gets hard as fired brick.

I then alighted and found my little home awaiting me. The tent-flaps tied open, the mattresses laid, the blankets turned back, the camp-table with candle-stick upon it, and a couple of camp-chairs at the door of the tent. Surely it is good to be in the army I then thought; and after a supper consisting of soldiers' hot biscuits, antelope steak broiled over the coals, and a large cup of black coffee, I went to rest, listening to the soughing of the pines.

—Martha Summerhayes
Camp Hualapais, 1874

Browned Flour

Used to thicken and darken gravy. Put flour in a hot oven or over a moderate fire, and stir it continually until it is brown. Do not scorch. Keep in tightly corked bottle or jar. When used, it should be combined with drippings or water.

Boiled Salt Pork

Soak pork overnight in cold water. Drain. Cover with cold water and boil in a covered pot. Turn pork several times and remove scum as it rises. As water evaporates, add boiling water and cook until done. If vegetables are available, they can be cooked with pork.

Although the officers of the command did not work with the axe and shovel as did the men, yet they had no advantage in the quality of the food on which they subsisted. They were allowed to purchase enough of it, such as it was. It was black coffee, dry bread, poor beef or poorer pork, with rice or beans, month after month, for a year and a half. Vegetables were never to be had at any place within two hundred miles. Potatoes and onions would have brought fabulous prices, could they have been obtained there. The Subsistence Department kept no stores for sale to officers except crushed sugar and, occasionally, poor hams and dried apples. For the first half bushel of potatoes I was able to buy in Arizona, I first paid sixteen dollars and would have given sixty had it been demanded. For once, money seemed to have lost nearly all its power. It could neither be eaten nor exchanged for that which the human system craved. When at last scurvy attacked the garrison, and the post surgeon demanded the purchase of anti-scorbutics, wagons were sent two hundred and fifty miles and loaded with onions at forty-five dollars per bushel, and potatoes and cucumber pickles at corresponding prices.

— Captain Camillus Carr
Camp McDowell, 1866

Baking Powder Biscuits

2 quarts sifted flour
1 large teaspoon salt
1 tablespoon drippings
    or lard

4 large teaspoons
    baking powder
cold water

Mix baking powder and salt into flour, and rub in the lard or drippings. Add enough cold water to make a soft dough. Handle dough as little as possible. Roll out dough into a sheet about 3/4 inch thick. Cut out circular cakes using biscuit cutter or empty can. Lay the cut biscuits close together in a well greased baking pan and bake 5 or 6 minutes in a hot oven until brown.

Fried Salt Pork

Cut pork into thin slices and soak in cold water about 1 hour. Drain and wipe dry. Fry pork in hot pan until brown on both sides. Season with pepper.

Dried Beef with Peppers

2 pounds jerked dried beef
browned flour
1 onion

2 ounces drippings
4 red peppers

Put beef in pan in hot oven for 10 minutes. Remove from oven and shred. Place in a frying pan with drippings and onion, and fry for about 5 minutes. Pour boiling water over the peppers and mash through a sieve and mix with beef. Then thicken with browned flour. Season to taste, cook for 20 minutes, and serve hot.

And now began our real journey up the Colorado River, that river unknown to me except in my early geographic lessons, and here we were, on the steamer "Gila," Captain Mellon, with the barge full of soldiers towing on after us, starting for Fort Mojave, some two hundred miles above.

We had staterooms, but could not remain in them long at a time, on account of the intense heat. I had never felt such heat, and no one else ever had or has since. The days were interminable. We wandered around the boat, first forward, then aft, to find a cool spot. We hung up our canteens (covered with flannel and dipped in water), where they would swing in the shade, thereby obtaining water which was a trifle cooler than the air. There was no ice, and consequently no fresh provisions: A Chinaman served as steward and cook, and at the ringing of a bell we all went into a small saloon back of the pilot-house, where the meals were served. Our party at table on the "Gila" consisted of several unmarried officers, and several officers with their wives, about eight or nine in all, and we could have had a merry time enough but for the awful heat, which destroyed both our good looks and our tempers. The fare was meager, of course; fresh biscuits without butter, very salty boiled beef, and some canned vegetables, which were poor enough in those days. Pies made from preserved peaches or plums generally followed this delectable course.

—Martha Summerhayes

Estufado

2 pounds beef ribs or mutton
1 tablespoon drippings
onions and peppers to taste
small amount of black pepper, minced garlic,
    tomatoes, and vinegar
4 slices toast

Combine all ingredients and stew slowly in covered pot until done. Serve on toast.

> *From Yuma to Ehrenberg the navigation of the river was easier. One day we saw a trapper coming down the river in a canoe; Captain Mellon called and asked him if he had any beavers' tails. He had, so the Captain laid in a supply and the next morning the Chinaman cook served them fried, along with buckwheat cakes; they were delicious and somewhat like pigs feet, only better.*
>
> —Diary of Mrs. William
>   Corbrusier, 1872

Pot Roast

Place brisket of beef in a kettle over a good fire. Add one pint of boiling water, cover, and cook slowly about 15 minutes for every pound of beef. Add some salt when meat is half done. When all the water evaporates, add no more since there should be enough fat in the kettle to finish cooking the meat. Serve with gravy made from the fat.

Bombshells

16 1/2 pounds meat
6 pounds flour
1 pound onions
3 ounces salt

1 ounce pepper
sweet herbs
water

Chop meat and onions into small pieces. Season with half the salt and pepper and all the herbs.

Add 1 1/2 pounds chopped beef fat and the remaining salt and pepper to the flour. Stir in enough water to make a stiff dough. Form dough into balls and roll out round. Put chopped meat into center and gather dough around like a dumpling. Tie dumpling in a floured pudding cloth and boil until done. This recipe feeds 22 men.

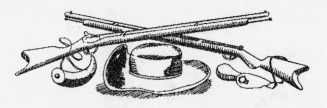

Vegetable Soup

4 pounds fresh beef
1 or 2 pounds soup bones
4 pounds available vegetables
1 gallon water
salt and pepper

Simmer meat and soup bone in water about 4 hours. Strain through a colander and return liquid and meat to pot. Cut vegetables into small pieces and add to soup. Simmer until tender. Remove vegetables, mash, and stir back into soup.

We messed together and as there was no one who could cook, I tried to instruct a soldier, which was a very difficult task while the wind was blowing the sand and smoke into one's face and into the food. We generally had coffee, eggs, bacon, bread and butter, condensed milk and hard bread for breakfast; canned meat, vegetables, bread and butter, coffee and canned fruit for dinner. The meals were served on a red and white tablecloth spread on the ground and we sat on boxes. Father, Claude and I each had a tin plate, cup, knife, fork, spoon and napkin, but the others managed somehow.

—Diary of Mrs. William Corbrusier
On the way to Camp Date Creek, 1873

Cannon Balls

6 pounds flour
1 1/2 pounds suet
3 pints molasses
1 pint water

Chop up suet and mix with flour. Then mix molasses and water together. Pour molasses mixture into flour and combine all ingredients. Mold into balls. Put each ball into a bag that has been dipped into boiling water, wrung out, and then floured inside. Make sure the ball has enough room to swell in the bag. Immerse bags in boiling water and cook for an hour or more until done. This recipe feeds 22 men.

ARMY SUPPLY LIST
Camp Verde 1889

OFFICERS

Canned Goods
Apples
Asparagus
Corn
Cranberry sauce
Lard
Milk
Mushrooms
Oysters
Pineapple
Salmon
Sardines
Tomatoes
Tongue
Peas

Dry Goods
Beans
Coffee
Corn meal
Corn starch
Flour
Gelatin
Macaroni
Oatmeal
Pepper
Powdered sugar
Rice
Salt
Soda crackers
Sugar
Tapioca
Tea
Wheat
Yeast powder

Miscellaneous
Butter
Cheese
Chocolate
Chowchow
Ham
Jam
Jelly
Lemon extract
Olives
Olive oil
Onions
Pickles
Pork
Potatoes
Syrup, maple
Vanilla extract
Vinegar
Worcestershire
   sauce

ENLISTED MEN

Canned Goods
Codfish
Corn
Corned beef
Cranberry sauce
Hominy
Jelly
Lard
Milk
Peaches
Tomatoes

Dry Goods
Allspice
Cinnamon
Brown sugar
Corn meal
Corn starch
Dried apples
Dried peaches
Flour
Macaroni
Oatmeal
Onions
Sugar, issue
Tea, mixed,
   black & green
Yeast powder

Miscellaneous
Bacon
Bottled gerkins
Butter
Ham
Lemon extract
Mustard
Potatoes
Raisins
Sweet potatoes
Syrup, golden
Vanilla extract

Lt. John Bigelow, Jr.
(1854-1936)

~~~
Historical
Profile
~~~

Lt. John Bigelow, Jr. graduated from West Point in 1877 as a second lieutenant and was assigned to the 10th United States Cavalry. By this time the Negro regiment had become a crack outfit of Indian fighters and had received its sobriquet, "The Buffalo Soldiers."

In 1885 the regiment's job under Bigelow was to help General Crook's efforts in bringing Apache warriors back from Mexico. The 10th Cavalry was to guard the mountain passes leading from Mexico to Arizona since no one knew where Geronimo and his band would strike.

Bigelow kept a careful journal of daily experiences as he and his comrades followed Geronimo since he hoped to sell an article based on the material to a national magazine. Many army officers during the 1870s and 1880s supplemented their pay in this way.

When the editor of Outing Magazine in New York read Bigelow's account, he was dazzled by the work and decided to run the journal in serial form from April to July of 1886 under the title, "On the Bloody Trail of Geronimo."

Frederick Remington, by the time of Bigelow's account, had gone west to portray Indians and military life but had not yet won fame and fortune as an illustrator.

When Remington walked into the same editor's office with a portfolio full of rough sketches, the editor not only bought the work but hired Remington to illustrate the Bigelow series. The job was Remington's first important commission.

In 1956 Westernlore Press resurrected Bigelow's work and published the series in book form along with all the illustrations. The press reissued the book in 1986.

In addition to the accounts quoted earlier in this cook book, the *journal carries many other references to the fare the men ate.*

Bigelow's entry for May 19, 1885, while in pursuit of Apaches read, "We ate our supper after dark, our tablecloth a piece of shelter tent, being laid on the ground by the cork fire. Our fierce appetites having finally succumbed to beans and bacon, we got up and stretched ourselves and then started out for camp headquarters."

On May 20th the group arrived at the San Simon rail station where the men managed a change from camp fare.

"We ate at the Traveler's Resort, the house of the flagman. Our meal consisted of one course: in the main, beef and potatoes. As we paid our 50 cents, the usual price for a western railroad meal, most of us thought we hardly got our money's worth. However, we did not know how long we might have to travel on salt meat and canned vegetables. Indeed, some of the officers had no canned vegetables. They fared on bread and bacon and coffee with an occasional mess of boiled beans. These were the few who followed to the letter the order given to us by the post commander, to take nothing but what we could carry on our horses."

It is important to note that Bigelow's account of the hardships of life in the Arizona desert did much to improve the enlisted man's lots, and that included a better diet!

Studio photo of an unidentified prospector.

Photo courtesy of Southwest Studies.

George Warren, *one of the early miners in the Bisbee area. A tragic figure, he never cashed in on Bisbee's wealth. The Town of Warren was named in his honor and his likeness graces the state seal of Arizona.*

Photo courtesy of Southwest Studies.

Miners

Mining in Arizona began in earnest during the 1850s when Charles Poston and Henry Ehrenberg opened up a string of silver mines near Tubac. Money poured in from Eastern investors, and a band of Mexican miners was contracted to work the rich veins. Prosperity seemed certain until United States troops were withdrawn from Arizona to fight the Civil War, and hostile Apaches then drove the workers back to Sonora and Tucson.

Meanwhile, in spite of Indian raids, Arizona's first gold rush was on. Indians, who had been picking up gold flakes and nuggets for years, told prospectors poking around Yuma that there was lots more of the glittering stuff on the Gila and Colorado rivers. Word first spread to California, and soon miners and prospectors, lured by stories of rich silver veins and gold placers, arrived in droves.

The trip from southern California was a hazardous trek from water hole to water hole across the inhospitable desert. From northern California, the trip was even more difficult. Miners boarded a steamer at San Francisco, sailed south around the Baja peninsula, and up the Gulf of California to Yuma.

But the hardships of travel and constant Apache raids didn't stop hardy old lizards like Ed Schieffelin, Pauline Weaver, and Henry Wickenburg from opening up new mining districts throughout the territory. Soon claims were being discovered and worked in Tombstone, along the Hassayampa River, and near Prescott. The era of the mining camp and boom town had come to stay, and excited prospectors began arriving from everywhere.

The fare of those first prospectors was monotonous at best. Each man took care of himself and carried what provisions he needed on the back of his pack mule—usually salt pork, flour, and beans.

Though silver and gold drew settlers first, copper mining began on a large scale about 1875. Soon the towns of Ajo, Clifton, Bisbee, Douglas, Jerome, and Globe were flourishing communities. The copper mines attracted Cornish miners, called "Cousin Jacks," and Irish immigrants by the late 1870s. These late arrivals had been frightened off at first by stories of Gila monsters, heat, and Apaches, but soon they made their way to the forbidding land to seek new homes and fortunes.

As the mining frontier expanded in the 1870s and 80s, stagecoach lines sprang up to serve the new districts. Stage stops had notoriously bad food. The coffee was too strong, the bread (if there was any) was too dry, and the salt pork and  beans were often rancid. Will Barnes reported on an eating station between Yuma and Tucson in 1880. After washing up in an Indian basket full of murky water, he dried his hands on a flour sack fastened to a tree nearby. Naturally, all the other travelers that day and for many days before had used the same facilities. The dining table was under a ramada roofed with willow boughs. Lizards scooted up and down the cottonwood support posts, and beetles and centipedes sometimes dropped from the boughs into the bowls below. Two Yuma Indian boys tending the table lethargically swished away the cloud of flies. Several women knelt over cooking fires nearby.

Dinner that day was chili con carne served in a big pottery bowl. Barnes wrote: "The old-timers at the table filled their plates with the stew, then spooned a lot of red ground material into it. The name 'chili' meant nothing in my young life, but I was willing to try anything once, especially when I was as hungry as I was then." He helped himself to a big plateful, all right, and stuffed his mouth with the first bite. It was darn hot chili. His eyes bulged and watered. He gasped and tried to

swallow, and the liquid fire seared his throat. Apparently Barnes and an Irish miner were the only two greenhorns at the table. The miner, who was as shocked at his first encounter with chili as Barnes, took the piece of meat out of his mouth, laid it aside, and remarked that he'd use it later to light his pipe.

Life in the mining camps was rough and hazardous at first. Miners were harassed by Indians, the weather, and each other. Prospectors camped out in the hills, or lived in tents or clapboard shacks. After a hard day of picking and mucking, the miner returned to camp for an uninviting meal of coffee, beans, and bacon. Then he'd go into town to drink in drafty saloons and fall easy prey to gambling swindles and shady ladies.

Some towns, such as Prescott, Jerome, Bisbee, and Tombstone, boomed in a big way and blossomed into communities complete with courthouses, restaurants, and civic pride. Schools, churches, newspapers, theaters, and other signs of civility replaced, or at least accompanied, the dreary gambling dens and dance halls. Life became a dramatic contrast between the luxury made possible by the mines and the harshness of the frontier environment. A Bisbee resident, for example, might dine on oysters and imported champagne at the Copper Queen Hotel at noon, and later watch the local school children scramble up a nearby hill and take cover during an "Apache drill."

Better hotels, restaurants, and boarding houses in the big mining towns began serving fine delicacies. Tombstonians loved to eat well. The (Tombstone) *Epitaph* ran news columns and advertisements about the tasty morsels at last week's party or the menus of the Russ House or Can Can Restaurant. Fish arrived regularly on ice from the Gulf of California, and imported foods came in from San Francisco long before the railroad ever got to Arizona. Prescott's favorite dishes included raisins, apple juice, and ice cream, not to mention fresh oysters on ice direct from Baltimore.

Little wonder the lone grubstaker with only a bagful of beans and flour was lured into town and parted from his money for a fine tasty meal!

Can Can Restaurant, Tombstone, 1880s.

Photo courtesy of Arizona Historical Society

Miner's Bread

2 cups flour
4 tablespoons bacon drippings or melted lard
1/2 teaspoon salt
1 tablespoon baking powder
1/2 cup water
1/2 cup canned milk
1 egg if available

Mix all ingredients together, and pour dough into greased baking pan. Bake till done in moderate oven. This bread busts better than it slices.

— *Jean Nuttall*

Oysters in Blankets

Roll each oyster in a slice of thin bacon. Fasten with a toothpick. Cook in a hot frying pan until bacon is crisp. Pour off the drippings as they accumulate. Serve on fingers of crisp toast.

— *Mrs. W. F. Dinney*

Hall and Poe of the Tragic Meat Market on Montezuma St. are in receipt of the finest and fattest fresh eastern oysters ever brought to Prescott. Send in your orders for the coming holidays.

— Arizona (Prescott) Journal Miner, 1883

Oyster Cocktail

3 teaspoons horseradish
3 teaspoons vinegar
5 teaspoons lemon juice
1/2 teaspoon Tabasco sauce
1 pint oysters
salt to taste

Mix all ingredients together and serve in tall thin glasses. This recipe serves six.

— *Mrs. Roy Perkins*

Fried Oysters

Wipe oysters dry and season well with salt and pepper. Dip in egg and cracker crumbs. Drop in deep fat and fry until brown.

— *Mrs. Dan Bradley*

Spanish Tongue

Cook tongue until tender. Then peel and simmer in a sauce of one can tomatoes, chopped onion, chopped green chile (peeled and seeded), and salt.

—*Mrs. A. V. Wagner*

Camp Fried Potatoes

Peel, quarter, and slice as many potatoes as needed. For each potato, use 1/4 cup flour, 1/2 teaspoon salt, and several shakes of pepper. Put potatoes, flour, and seasoning in paper sack, and shake up. Fry in hot lard or drippings.

—*Jean Nuttall*

McKenzie and Doverney are prepared to accommodate regular boarders at the New Arcade at the rate of $10.00 per week. Their customers, in addition to having the advantage of fresh fish, oysters, game and all the delicacies of the season, cooked to order, may be sure of being satisfied as Bill Doverney, the well known caterer, will be in charge, with Charley Gray, Prescott's favorite waiter, as head steward.

— Arizona (Prescott) Journal Miner, 1883

Roast Suckling Pig

Clean piglet. Do not remove head or feet. Make a stuffing of dry bread, grated onion, sage, salt, pepper, and warm water for moisture. Fill the cavity with stuffing and sew closed. Stand pig in pan of water, beef stock, onion, and butter and baste often. Bake slowly for three hours. Put a corn cob in his mouth and serve hot with baked apples.

Menu

THANKSGIVING DINNER

Maison Doree Restaurant

SOUP

Chicken Gumbo

FISH

Tenderloin of Sole-Tartar Sauce

ENTREES

Buffalo Tongue • Papillote
Saddle of lamb a la Milanese
Pate Financiere

VEGETABLES

String Beans   Corn   French Peas

ROAST

Turkey, Cranberry Sauce
Suckling Pig, Apple Sauce
Beef • Lamb

SALAD

Celery • Lettuce

ENTREMETS

Queen Fritters, a l'Israelite
Cream Puffs, Vanilla

PASTRY

Custard Pie • Mince Pie • Apple Pie • Cranberry Pie

DESSERT

Fruit • Walnuts • Almonds etc. etc.

— Tombstone Epitaph, 1887

Roast Quail or Wild Turkey

Wash fowl in cold water and sprinkle with a mixture of flour, salt, and pepper. Bake for 2 hours in a quart of water in a covered roaster. Then pour broth into stuffing for moisture. StuJI fowl, and cook in oven I more hour.

-Mrs. J. F. Daggs

Broiled Venison Steak

Place the venison steak on a hot broiler. When partially cooked, tum and season with salt and pepper. When both sides are seasoned and cooked, remove from fire and brush with butter. Serve hot with baked potatoes.

-E1i~abelh H"ll

The Juniper House, Prescott's first hotel, opened July 4, 1864. The bill-of-fare that day was the following:

Breakfast

Fried Venison and Chili

Bread and Coffee with Milk

Dinner

Roast Venison and Chili

Chili Baked Beans

Chili and Tortillas

Tea and Coffee with Milk

Venison with Chili

Cut 1 pound venison steak into cubes and throw into pan with hot lard. Fry until brown. Add 2 cups water and 1 tablespoon flour to thicken. Add a teaspoon of ground chili, and salt and pepper to taste. Simmer until done.

—Mrs. A. Willson

Good Potato Soup

Fry some bacon. Add 2 or 3 medium-sized potatoes that have been cubed. Add enough water to cover. Simmer until tender. Then add salt, butter, and about a cup or more of milk, and bring just to a boil.

—*Louise Kinkead*

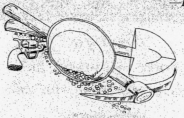

Corned Beef Hash

1 can corned beef
3 fairly good-sized potatoes
1 large onion
1 green chile, peeled and seeded
salt

Slice potatoes and fry in bacon or ham grease. When potatoes are half done, add sliced onion and chopped chili. Then cut up corned beef and add to mixture. Stir well and continue cooking until potatoes are tender. Delicious with baking powder biscuits.

—*Gertrude Curtis*

> *Game as wild as a tornado, chicken as tender as a maiden's heart, ice cream as delicious as a day in June, dessert that would charm the soul of a South Sea Islander and smiles as bright as the morning sun will be found at the Can Can (Restaurant) today.*
>
> —*Tombstone Epitaph, 1880s*

Cornish Pasties

Crust for 8 large pasties:
- **2 cups suet put through meat grinder or 1 cup lard**
- **3 cups flour**
- **1 teaspoon baking powder**
- **1 teaspoon salt**
- **cold water**

Blend all ingredients thoroughly and add just enough water to hold the dough together. Then divide the dough into 8 portions and roll each out separately.

Filling:
- **2 pounds diced round steak or other meat**
- **3/4 pound diced lean pork**
- **6 cups chopped raw potatoes**
- **1 cup chopped raw turnips**
- **1 sliced onion**
- **salt and pepper**
- **butter or marrow**

Cover half of each rolled out pastry with the filling. Dot well with butter or marrow, and then fold the dough over and crimp edges together. Bake 1 hour at 350 degrees.

Pasties were a favorite food of the Cornish miners who came to Arizona, and the meat pie was the main food carried in their metal lunch pails.

— Mabel Iater

Batter Pudding

1 cup butter
1 cup sugar
2 eggs
1 cup milk
2 heaping cups flour
1 teaspoon baking powder

Combine all ingredients and mix well. Bake in moderate oven until done. Serve with sauce.

Spotted Dog

(Raisin Cake)

1 1/2 cups flour
1 cup sugar
1/2 cup butter
2 eggs
1 cup milk or water
1 teaspoon lemon flavoring
1/2 cup raisins
2 teaspoons baking powder

Cream butter, and add sugar and both egg yolks. Next add the lemon flavoring and liquid. Mix well. Pour into sifted flour and baking powder. Drop raisins into flour before mixing so they don't sink. Whip egg whites and fold in. Bake till straw comes out clean. This cake is good with or without frosting.

— Jean Nuttall

Wagoner Vinegar Pie

3/4 cup sugar
1/4 cup flour
1/2 teaspoon salt
1 teaspoon cinnamon
1/4 teaspoon cloves

1/4 teaspoon allspice
1 1/2 cups hot water
3 tablespoons vinegar
2 tablespoons butter
3 beaten eggs

Mix the sugar, flour, salt, and spices together. Then add the water, vinegar, butter, and eggs. Cook over low heat until mixture thickens. Pour filling into a pie shell which has been baked 2 or 3 minutes in a hot oven. Bake pie 30 minutes in a moderate oven.

Cranberry Pie

1/2 cup sugar
1/2 cup corn starch
1 cup water
1/2 cup molasses
1 quart cranberries, finely chopped
1/2 teaspoon salt

Mix corn starch, sugar, and water and bring to a boil. Then add molasses, cranberries, and salt. This makes enough filling for two pies with upper and lower crusts.

Never Fail Pie Crust

3 cups flour
1/2 teaspoon baking powder
1/2 cup lard
1/2 cup butter
1/2 cup ice water
pinch salt

Mix dry ingredients and then add water. Mix and roll out. Double over and roll out several times as this makes the dough flaky.

—*Mrs. George Barney*

Stella Hughes

(1916-   )

Stella Hughes has cooked over a lot of fires for a lot of Arizona cowboys, and has talked to "old-timers who wandered in the mysteries of chuck wagon cooking all their lives," she said.

Her mother was a prodigious canner and preserver of foods on the Oklahoma farm where she was born. "I might have learned a lot from her if I'd not been so set on being a cowgirl," she recalled. But as the years went by, she became an accomplished horse-woman who participated in rodeos in Salinas, Bakersfield, and Los Angeles during the 1930s.

Her first extended visit to Arizona was a trip to the Tonto Basin in 1931. "Here I ate my first dried apple pie, sweetened with wild honey, with a rich flaky crust made from rendered bear fat. It was pure ambrosia...no, it wasn't. It was the best derned apple pie I ever ate," she exclaimed.

In 1938 she married Mack Hughes, an Arizona cowman, the genuine article, and her education in ranch cooking began in earnest.

That first eventful year she was expected to feed the crew on a cow outfit located on the edge of the Navajo Reservation. "On roundups there were dust storms, alkali water (or none at all), unsuitable wood (or none at all), heat, flies...and a relentless wind that blows 13 months of the year. Twelve months of the year it blows real hard." She went on to explain that the only "conveniences" in that particular cow camp were a wood burning stove and a windmill 100 yards away (meaning there was no running water).

Even before her marriage she began collecting dutch oven

recipes and racked up a respectable collection of cook's tales and home remedies, which she called "Rx for man and horse."

Later, Mack served as stockman for the IDT herd on the Apache Reservation where the couple lived for several decades 75 miles from San Carlos. During those years Stella honed her dutch oven skills under the tutelage of Apache cooks, the connoisseurs of hardwood coal cookery.

From the Mexican horsebreakers who worked with Mack she learned how to pit barbecue everything from beef to beans to turkey filled with stuffing.

Each year when Mack took the herd to market, Stella went along on the drive, "but not as cook!" she said. "Oh, I was on standby in case the cook quit (which they nearly always do before the cattle are shipped), but I drove the cattle all the way and said fervent prayers each day that the cook stayed until the drive was over. Truly there is no harder job than slinging heavy dutch ovens and preparing meals for 20 men over an open fire."

Mack retired in 1974 and since then the couple has lived on their own ranch on Eagle Creek near Clifton, Arizona.

Stella has preserved her knowledge of old time recipes in Chuck Wagon Cookin' (U of A Press, 1974), Hashknife Cowboy— Recollections of Mack Hughes (U of A Press 1984), an authentic account of ranch life in the fading days of the old west and Bacon and Beans, Ranch-Country Recipes (Western Horseman Inc., 1990).

Stella contributed material and coached the author through the section of cowcamp cooking in this book.

Cowboys

Father Kino was Arizona's first cattleman. Besides tending souls and establishing missions, he set up ranches in northern Sonora and southern Arizona as early as 1700.

Later, to encourage settlement of the northern frontier lands, the Spanish rulers gave their friends huge land grants. Haciendas, surrounded by rich rangeland and gardens, prospered in southern Arizona from about 1790 to 1815. But Indian hostilities brought the era to a tragic close. Ranching in the area didn't revive until the 1850s, when the pioneer Pete Kitchen established his fortified ranch near present-day Nogales. He defied the Apaches in battle after battle, and in spite of their constant raids he raised cattle, grains, fruits, cabbages, and potatoes. His prized hams, which he personally raised and cured, graced tables from Nogales to Silver City, New Mexico.

By the late 1870s, ranchers were drifting in from Utah,

Cowboy cooking included such essentials as beans,
coffee, flour and salt

Photo courtesy of Southwest Studies

Cooking in a Cochise County cowcamp.

Photo courtesy of Special Collections, University of Arizona

California, New Mexico, and Texas. Though barbed wire and homesteaders had broken up the open range elsewhere, Arizona's grass grew high as a horse's belly, and the land was free, unstocked, and unfenced.

Longhorns were the principal breed of cattle in those days. These lanky cattle, descendants of the early Spanish stock, seemed to thrive on adversity. They survived not only drought and blizzard, but also their thorny desert diet. Unfortunately, the meat was lean and tough and not particularly palatable to the denizens of the mining camps and military posts where it was marketed. By the 1880s pioneer ranchmen were building up their stock by introducing new breeds of cattle.

With the larger herds came the cowboys, and with the cowboys came a distinctive lifestyle. It was in the roundup camp that legendary cooks and cookery won their fame.

Much as Arizonans hate to admit it, an ingenious Texan invented the chuck wagon. The brainstorm hit pioneer cattleman Charles Goodnight in 1866 before the first long cattle drive from Texas to the Kansas railroad. He figured the trip would take awhile and the cowboys would get cranky as mad rattlers without good grub, so he rustled up an iron-axled government wagon left over from the Civil War and transformed it into a rolling kitchen.

Goodnight nailed a tall chuck box on the back of the wagon and fitted it with a drop door that let down to make a table. The box was a miracle of utility, with shelves and drawers inside for storing everything the potwrangler needed. Each essential of camp cookery had a niche—the sourdough keg, coffee, salt, salt pork, beans, flour, dried fruit, molasses, lard, onions, and all the clattering tin plates, cups, and eating irons. Under the box was a rack for the dutch ovens, frying pans, and coffee pot, and beneath the wagon itself was a cowhide sling filled with wood and cow chips for the cooking fire. The wagon's utility didn't stop with cooking supplies. The cowboys' bedrolls, water kegs, shovels, axes, and branding irons filled the mid-section of the wagon, and a smaller box up front held small tools and horseshoe nails.

The chuck wagon, San Carlos Indian Reservation, 1909.
Photo courtesy of Special Collections, University of Arizona

The first chuck wagon was a lumbering creation pulled by ten yoke of oxen, an ill soon remedied by the cowpunchers, who figured horses or mules were better suited to the job.

Although individual cooks would change a detail here and there, the basic design and function of the chuck wagon remained the same. In Arizona Territory, cooks would usually attach a waterproof tarp to the back of the wagon that could be spread over the working area in case of rain.

The camp cook himself was a notorious conjurer. Most cowboys claimed they never knew any but the mean-tempered sort. But the wonder of heavenly stews simmering in the dutch oven and golden brown biscuits kept the hands respectful. The cook was the most important member of the outfit's crew, bar none. He drew twice the cowboy's wages and usually determined the success or failure of a roundup. He was up by three every morning and managed to keep coffee on the embers and prepare a meal come rain, stampede, or blinding dust.

The cook's best concoctions were often a result of his uncanny ability to make do. From the limited supplies in his chuck box, a good cook could produce such wonders as raisin pudding, dried apple pie, and doughnuts. But the mainstays of cowcamp cooking were sourdough, beef, and beans.

Sourdough was an indispensable part of every meal. A cowboy just didn't feel fed unless sourdough biscuits, bread, or pancakes had been part of the fare. The starter was kept in a wooden keg, a crock, or a lard pail. The wooden keg was usually preferred because it was sturdy, and a fussy cook could wrap it up and take it to bed on cold nights to help the fermenting process along.

Beef stews were cooked in a dutch oven, which was both a necessity and a tradition because the cooking method tenderized the meat. The only vegetables that ever ended up in the stew pot were potatoes and onions, and an occasional can of tomatoes—and only because they kept well. Green vegetables were hearsay and considered unworthy of masculine attention by the cowboys.

Besides stew, the cowboys liked steak dipped in flour and fried in the dutch oven. This might have been the main course for any meal of the day. And then there was jerky. The cook sometimes pounded the dried beef, browned the flakes in fat and flour, added water, and then ladled the gravy over sourdough biscuits or potatoes. Jerky was also cooked with pinto beans in the graniteware beanpot, or munched by itself.

In Arizona there was no bean but the pinto. The cowboy, no doubt, would have snarled with contempt at any other but this speckled brown and white bean. He liked pintos with chili, salt pork, or beef, ladled over biscuits, or fresh out of the beanhole.

No chapter on cowcamp cooking would be complete without mentioning the cowboys' favorite dish, son-of-a_____ stew. No one knows just who originated the recipe or why it bears that name, but the general consensus is that the fixings included all but the hoofs, horns, and hide.

The stew sometimes went by other names. If women were present, the cowboys politely referred to it as son-of-a-gun stew. They might also name it after some individual in particular disfavor at the time. The name could last a whole season or for only one meal, but always the implication was obvious. Cooks were known to be fired for calling the stew by the boss' name.

There were as many recipes as cooks. Some used water, and others claimed that only the natural juices could produce the right flavor. Some cooks grew pale at the thought of adding onions to the brew, and some insisted it wasn't authentic without them. Then there was the argument that the stew was better the second day. This debate was quickly shelved, though, because there never was any left over. On one point they agreed. A son-of-a-gun could have no heart and no brains, but it wasn't a son-of-a-gun without guts. This essential ingredient, the marrow gut, is part of the small intestine. When cooked with the heart, tongue, sweetbreads, kidneys, liver, and brains, it provided the distinctive flavor of the stew.

The Dutch Oven and How to Use It

The first dutch ovens were brought to America by the Pilgrims, but when folks started moving west, they brought the versatile cooking vessel along.

A real dutch oven is made of heavy cast iron, has stubby legs, a bail, and a lid with a turned-up rim for holding coals. Anything else is an impostor. The best place to hunt for one today is in an old-fashioned southwestern hardware store. The shallow variety is best for making breads, biscuits, and desserts, and deep ovens are for stews and roasts.

Now let's cook. Build a fire at least an hour before starting the food. Dig a hole and gather some good hard wood. Use mesquite or oak because pine won't burn down into good cooking embers. When you have a pit full of coals, break them up so they are all pretty much the same size. Then put a heaping shovelful of coals on level ground.

For biscuits, warm the dutch oven and grease the insides. Meanwhile, let the lid heat up hot. You'll need a pothook or some equivalent of your own invention to lift it. Pinch off hunks of dough and arrange them in the oven. Put the lid on, set the dutch oven in the pile of coals, and heap more coals over the lid. The coals will be hotter in some places than others, so rotate the oven by its bail a few times during baking. Peek once to see how the biscuits are getting along. If they are browning too fast on top, dump the embers off the lid. In about fifteen minutes the biscuits will be done just right.

The cowcamp cooks and pioneers proved that absolutely anything can be cooked in a dutch oven, whether it be fried steak, cobbler, or stew. With practice even pies can be baked by putting the pie pan on three rocks inside the dutch oven to keep the bottom crust from burning.

Many of the recipes in this section are for dutch ovens, though they can also be cooked on a stove.

Dutch Oven Biscuits

6 cups flour
3 teaspoons salt
4 1/2 teaspoons baking powder
3/4 cup lard or bacon grease

Mix ingredients with enough diluted evaporated milk to make a batter that can be pinched without sticking to the hands. Put about 1/4 inch melted grease in bottom of dutch oven.

Pinch off hunks of dough, dip them in hot grease, and arrange in oven, greased side up, for golden brown biscuits. This recipe is for a large dutch oven.

And when you're tired and hungry, fancy food don't mean a thing. Jes' give us meat an' biscuits an' black coffee with a sting.

Sourdough Starter

Put 1 pint flour in a pail with a lid. Add 2 tablespoons sugar and 1 tablespoon salt. Mix well. Stir in 1 1/2 cups water and beat to a smooth dough. Add 1 tablespoon vinegar to the batter, and set in warm place to sour. When it smells real sour, it is ready to use.

Or, after you have boiled potatoes, save the water. Add 4 cups flour, 2 teaspoons salt, and 2 teaspoons sugar to 4 cups potato water and blend well. Put in covered crock or keg, and set in warm place for several days to ferment.

Sourdough Pancakes

Put at least 1 cup of sourdough starter in a large mixing bowl, large enough to allow batter to rise. Add 2 cups of lukewarm water and about 2 1/2 cups of flour. Mix thoroughly. Cover bowl and set in a warm place overnight.

Next morning add:

1 egg
2 tablespoons oil or bacon drippings
1/4 cup milk

Mix into batter well, then add:

1 teaspoon salt
1 teaspoon baking soda
2 tablespoons sugar

Blend salt, soda, and sugar into a smooth dry mixture, and sprinkle over top of batter and fold in gently. This will cause a slight foaming action. Fry on hot, lightly greased griddle. If batter is too thick, thin with a small amount of milk.

Sourdough pancakes need a hotter griddle than ordinary pancakes. To make cornmeal pancakes, use 1/4 cup cornmeal and eliminate 1/4 cup of flour.

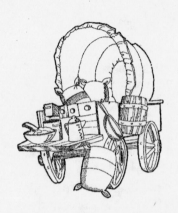

Beefsteak Pudding

Four cups prepared flour, 1 cup cold water, 1/2 cup suet, 2 pounds round steak cut into pieces as for stewing, pepper, salt, and ketchup.

Free the suet from strings and rub it to powder. Chop it into the flour. Add a pinch of salt, and work with the water into a paste just stiff enough to be handled. Butter the inside of a round plain bowl, and line it with the paste. The paste should not be over 1 inch thick. Fill with the cut meat, sprinkling each layer with pepper, and salt, and dashes of ketchup. Cover the top with a piece of pastry cut to fit it. Tie over all a good-sized pudding-cloth, floured liberally on the inside, and fasten securely, but not so tightly as to hinder the swelling of the pastry. Set the mold in a pot with boiling water enough to cover it well. Boil hard for 2 hours, taking care that the water is filled up as fast as it boils away.

When it is done, plunge it upside down for a few seconds in cold water until the cloth slips off. Put a dish under the inverted mold and turn the pudding out upon it.

Son-of-a-Gun Stew

1/2 the heart
1/2 the melt
1/4 the liver
all the sweetbreads
all the butcher's steak

3 feet marrow gut
2 cups rendered leaf fat
1 minced garlic clove
1 set of brains

Cut the heart, liver, sweetbreads, melt, and butcher's steak into small cubes. The marrow gut should be cut into pieces about an inch long. Combine the above ingredients and season with salt and pepper. Then dredge with flour. When rendered fat has been well heated in a heavy skillet or dutch oven, add the meat and fry until brown. Add boiling water to cover, and garlic. Cook slowly for an hour or so. Add the brains (rinsed and broken), and continue cooking one more hour. This recipe will feed 12 to 15 hungry cowboys.

This stew has as many variations as names. Some cooks skinned and cubed the tongue. Many omitted the melt (a ductless gland located near the floating kidney), and others added onions.

But whether it was called Rascal, The Gentleman from El Paso, or Boss Man Stew, it was the cowboy's own favorite dish.

Pit Barbecue

To barbecue half a beef, first dig a pit 5 feet deep, 3 feet wide, and 6 feet long. The evening before the barbecue, build a fire in the pit using about a cord of dry mesquite or oak wood. The next morning, pull out any charred logs. Be sure you have about 18 inches of good red coals in the pit.

Cut the meat into 10-pound roasts and rub each with oil. Then sprinkle with chili powder, salt, and pepper. Put chopped garlic and onion slices on top, and wrap meat securely in cheese cloth. Rustle up some burlap feed bags, and wrap each roast individually. Tie securely with wire. Dip burlap bundles in water.

Put a light layer of dirt over the coals so the meat won't burn. Arrange the bundles in the pit, making sure they do not touch. Then cover with a light layer of dirt. Next, add a layer of hot rocks to keep in the heat. Fill the pit with dirt and pack down hard so no smoke escapes. Cook 8 to 10 hours.

I recall the first roundup I attended about the age of five; my mother would help me onto a pony as soon as the bellowing could be heard as the cattle neared the roundup ground, and I would ride out to watch the branding, roping, and all the other exciting things that happened, and last but not least, to eat at noon with the cowboys and see the huge beanpot full of beans and the dutch ovens of delicious meat.

— Dave Hopkins

Beanhole Beans

Beforehand: Dig a hole about 2 feet deep and a little wider. Burn hard wood, such as oak or mesquite, down to embers. Be sure hole is dried out and there are about 8 inches of good red coals.

2 cups pinto beans
1/2 pound salt pork
fresh garlic
salt and pepper
1 1/2 quarts water

Wash beans well. Then put all ingredients into a pot with a tight-fitting lid, and bring to a boil over open fire. Now put the beanpot into the hole, and pile embers on top. Cover with dirt, and pat down well so heat can't escape. Leave the beans in the hole all day long, and excavate before supper. A lard bucket or graniteware vessel makes an ideal beanpot.

And then we'd have, oh sometimes we'd have canned stuff—canned vegetables, and the old-time cowboys would call the canned goods "airtights." "Open an airtight." Well, that'd be a can of tomatoes, or a can of peaches, or whatever.

—— Gail Gardner

Cowcamp Stew

5 pounds stew meat
2 large onions
10 potatoes
2 large cans tomatoes
salt and pepper

Cut up stew meat in small pieces and brown in fat until all is nicely seared. Add onions diced fine, and water to cover. Let simmer until almost done. Add potatoes cut up in chunks and then salt and pepper. When done, add tomatoes and simmer 15 minutes. Cowcamps seldom, if ever, had fresh vegetables, and even onions and potatoes were a luxury most of the time.

Another way: Stew meat as above and add onions, 2 cups rice, and 2 cups macaroni instead of potatoes.

A cowcamp stew was usually made from anything at hand. Some would put in a can of every kind of vegetable on hand such as corn, peas, tomatoes, or hominy. We called this a mulligan stew and some called it slum-gullion.

— *Stella Hughes*

Fried Marrow Gut

Unbraid marrow gut and rinse well. Then cook in salted water until skin can be pierced with a fork. Do not cut it before cooking, as that will cause you to lose all the marrow. When it is done, take it out and cut into pieces 1 1/2 inches long. Roll in flour and fry in fat until brown. It has oysters skinned a mile for flavor.

— *Dora Sessions*

Corn Dodgers

Mix 4 cups whole ground cornmeal, 1 teaspoon salt, and 1 tablespoon melted lard or bacon drippings. Add enough boiling water to make a good stiff dough. Mold into cakes and bake in a greased dutch oven until brown.

Cowboys ate these hot out of the oven or packed them along for a meal with jerky and coffee. When corn dodgers got hard and stale, they could be mixed with water and made into mush.

Potato Doughnuts

2 medium potatoes
2 tablespoons lard or good clean drippings
2 well-beaten eggs
1 1/2 cups sugar
1 gill (1/2 cup) milk
3 teaspoons baking powder
5 cups flour

Boil and mash potatoes. Stir in lard while potatoes are still hot. Then add eggs, sugar, milk, and the flour that has been sifted with the baking powder. Knead more flour in on board if necessary. Cut and fry in deep fat. Makes a bunch.

— *Clair Haight*

And then, we'd always have some rice, and you'd make what the cowboys would call a "pie." A pie was rice and raisins. You just take dried raisins and cook the rice up and dump the raisins in, or you can do it with dried apricots either; cause that's one thing you'd use, and cowboys got to callin' that a pie. "We'll make a pie"; well, that's rice and raisins.

— Gail Gardner

Dutch Oven Rice Pudding with Fruit

4 cups cold cooked rice
2 cups sugar
2 cups dried cooked apricots, peaches, or
apples
1 cup boiling water

In dutch oven, start with layer of fruit and alternate layers with rice, sprinkling each layer with sugar. Pour the water over the top and bake in dutch oven with medium coals until done.

Double this recipe for round-up crew of 10 to 12 men.

Dutch Oven Bread Pudding

I used to make a bread pudding the cowboys liked out of cold sourdough biscuits, 2 or 4 days old, broken up. Stir it up soft, put in cooked raisins or prunes or dried cooked apples, sweeten heavy and mix with some canned milk. Don't cook too dry, just gooey. Top it off with a white sauce flavored with vanilla or cinnamon.

— *Slim Ellison*

Historical Profile

Slim Ellison

(1891-1983)

Slim Ellison must have been eight feet tall, or so it seemed to me when we met in Globe in 1975. He towered in his huge white Stetson and a horsehair bolo hung around his neck. He was 84 years old then, a living legend, and not an historian, but one who made history on the ranches and ranges he called home.

He had been a well-known cowboy, camp cook, trail driver and rancher since the turn of the century in Mogollon Rim country north of Globe. When he taught me how to cook biscuits in a dutch oven on a trip to his old homestead on Cherry Creek, I figured I got the information from the original source, so to speak. He became friends with our family and was happy to contribute recipes and information used in this book.

Slim's grandfather build a prosperous ranch on the Tonto Basin in 1885, but Slim's dad was a wanderer. Slim's formal education stopped somewhere in the fourth grade which did not hinder the University of Arizona Press' opinion of two books he authored late in life, both recollections of ranch life in Mogollon Rim country.

The family's wanderings gave Slim a thorough knowledge of the land and individuals who settled it. He had a remarkable memory of incidents that occurred throughout his life and a colorful way of relating stories using ranch lingo and a system of spelling uniquely his own.

Though the U of A Press published Cowboys Under the Mogollon Rim (1968) and More Tales from Slim Ellison (1981), Slim was not satisfied. All those over-educated people edited the soul out of his work, he complained. They cleaned up his spelling, punctuation and grammar to such a degree that he did not recognize the books as his own. (With all due respect to the press, they honestly tried to keep the spirit of the stories and the story teller intact, but Slim was greatly offended nonetheless.)

With ire in his eyes, Slim wrote a third book of recollections in 1975 called Back Trackin. The small paperback was privately printed in Globe in an edition of 1,000 copies.

"This little book writ by me has not been edited and is jist like I writ it & the way I wanted it—," he explained.

Here is a description of an old-time cow camp breakfast told HIS way:

Jist B-4 day break old greasy, The Cook, rolls out of his Soogans Bed on the ground—Starts a fire—Piles on some oak wood—Fills a 2 gal Coffee Pot with water, sometimes muddy, sometimes tastes Cattle—Dumps in a Cup or 2 ground coffee, sets the Pot near fire or against it—If he puts it on the fire, the wood settles & Pot Turns over—He puts a 16 in Dutch oven lid on the fire, sets the oven on Top—Turns a pack box on its side & cuts some steak—Puts flour enuff in a pan to make Biskits for 10 men—Puts in 2 Tablespoon heapin of Bakin Powder & Some salt & some lard for shortening & water to make soft Dough—Gets oven off fire Pots grease enuff to grease a Biskit on each side as he makes & puts em in—The fire by now has Pretty well burned down to coals—He shovels out some on the ground, sets oven on em, lifts Hot lid off fire with a hook, puts it on oven, covers lid with coals—By then Breakin day & coffee has biled—He shakes the wranglers quietly and Sez Come out of the nest and Jingle the ponys—Sets another oven on the fire & levels it—Put in Beef Tallow or lard about 2 in deep—Salt, Pepper on stk—Rolls it in flour & flops it into the oven—Has a pot of stewed dry apples & raisins—

Every thing sets on the ground except plates etc—He has them on side of a layin down Pack Box or in a Dish Pan—Lifts the oven lid—Biskits Brown—Steaks Done—

He Squawls out, Come A live U Sorry stock Disturbers & fill UR Rotters—(Different Cooks give Different calls)—The cowboys come & help their Selves—Theres generaly a can of lick (syrup) if they want it—When cowboys finish They drop dishes in a Dish Pan Called round up—

Slim Ellison died in Globe, Arizona, August 5, 1983 at the age of 91, and with him, the memories of a past era.

Mormons

The 1870s was a period of expansion for the Mormon church, a time of putting down new roots and spreading religion to souls who lived in the wilderness. Before the first ox-drawn wagons rolled southward from Utah, the land of the Little Colorado River in northeastern Arizona had been explored by Mormon scouts. The land was good for farming, they reported, and soon two hundred missionary families loaded up their belongings and began the arduous trip to Arizona.

Hardships were not new to the Mormons. Many had already crossed the continent in wagons and knew what to expect of life on the trail. Packing was the first order of business after one procured a good team and wagon. One bachelor's packing list included two barrels of nails, a frying pan, bucket, tin plates and cups, a hoe, pitchfork, and rifle. Besides the hardware, he took four bushels of wheat, one bushel of potatoes, five hundred pounds of flour, forty gallons of molasses, twenty pounds of apples, one ham, six pounds of butter, candles, soap, matches, and garden seeds.

Some pioneers took luxuries or family heirlooms, but such nonessentials as pianos, organs, wood stoves, and sewing machines often had to be abandoned along the trail to lighten the wagons.

The road from southern Utah to the Arizona border was smooth and worn, but beyond that lay the exhausting trek into the new territory. In the winter, the trail was buried under drifts of snow, and the animals' feet froze. The Colorado River crossing at Lee's Ferry was another peril of the journey. Wagons, cattle, and draft animals were crowded on the rickety ferry deck, and sometimes the terrified beasts crashed overboard and had to swim

An Arizona Mormon pioneer family camps along the trail, 1906.
Photo courtesy of Calvin Bateman Collection

across the river. Hardships did not stop at the other shore. The steepest grade of the trip was just ahead. The pioneers had to either double their teams for the climb or unload the wagons and pack their belongings up the steep slope on their backs.

Finally they arrived at their destinations. The settlers spent their first months camped in wagon boxes while they cleared the land, built dams, and planted crops. Before the towns were built, the Mormons lived in huge forts complete with apartments, a council house, community dining hall, kitchen, grist mill, and blacksmith shop. The fort compound also had chicken coops, cattle corrals, melon patches, and a large vegetable garden.

At the forts, the Mormons ate together at long tables in the communal dining hall. Women assigned to prepare the meals had a large variety of foods to choose from. While many of Arizona's other pioneers were subsisting on salt pork and beans, the Mormons were eating cheese and milk from their dairy herds, eggs from their laying hens, and produce from their gardens and orchards.

Survival in the desert was not always easy, however. Dams broke, floods and drought plagued the settlers, and crops often withered and died. But with singularity of purpose and determination, the Mormons built on.

Schools, brick homes, and cultivated fields soon dotted the land in every area the Mormons settled. Within a few years the towns of the Little Colorado as well as Safford, Lehi, Mesa, and St. David had become oases.

Ida Jesperson's Homemade Soap

6 pounds of animal fat
1 13-ounce can of lye
2 1/2 pints water

Heat grease until melted. The solid particles will either rise to the top (to be skimmed off) or sink to the bottom. Add the lye to the water in a porcelain or crockery vessel. Stir with a long-handled wooden spoon. Then add grease gradually to water and lye mixture, stirring occasionally several times until the mixture is the consistency of honey, about 15 minutes after adding fat, depending on air temperature.

Pour into containers. Let soap harden for several days. Can be grated or used in mesh bag for laundry.

— *Elma Jones*

> *"It must be acknowledged that the Mormons were wilderness breakers of high quality. They not only broke it, but they kept it broken; and instead of the gin mill and gambling hell as the cornerstones of their progress and as examples to the natives, they planted orchards, gardens, farms, schoolhouses and peaceful homes."*
>
> *— F. S. Dellenbaugh, 1909*

Mormon or Brigham Tea

(Ephedra)

My father said it was his responsibility as a child, when camp was made for the night, to look for the Brigham tea and get it into the big pot of water already set to boil on the campfire.

The greenish stems of this plant may be used fresh or dried. A handful of them in two or three pints of boiling water, then set aside to steep and sweetened with honey, is a delicious beverage. It is said to have many health-giving qualities.

—*Elma Jones*

Corn Casserole

3 cups corn cut from cobs
1/2 cup water
1 teaspoon salt

Cook 30 minutes on very low heat until corn is tender. Add 3/4 teaspoon dry mustard and a little cayenne, if you have it, for extra flavor. Beat 1 egg well, add 2 cups scalded milk and a little fat, also a little chopped onion, to the corn. Thicken with about 1/4 or 1/3 cup flour mixed with milk. Sprinkle with 1 cup buttered bread crumbs and bake in moderate oven for about 30 minutes or until the crumbs are golden brown.

Variation: Add some bacon, or pork cracklings, or pounded jerky just before putting in oven.

Sun-Dried Corn

Cook corn in salted boiling water for 5 minutes. When corn is cool enough to take in hands, cut down from cob with sharp knife. Spread kernels on trays (single layer), and cover with thin cloth. Leave trays in sun for several days but bring indoors at night. When kernels are completely dry, store in covered jars.

To cook: Soak about four hours, then boil until tender. Season with crisp bits of pork, or jerky, or a few pinches of red chile crumbled.

Jerky I

Trim all fat off meat. Cut meat into strips about 1 inch by 12 inches. Sprinkle all sides with salt. Sprinkle with pepper and/or chili if desired. Hang on wires in warm dry place. Full sun is best, but a barn loft will do if warm and dry. The clothesline is fine, but do not let meat get rained on. The salt will keep flies and bugs away.

When the meat feels and looks like leather, remove from wires and store in cool place in flour sacks. It can also be left hanging from rafters away from weevils and mice, in a cool place.

Jerky II

2 cups corn meal
5 tablespoons salt
4 tablespoons pepper (black)
4 tablespoons chili powder

Roll strips of meat in mixture. Hang on clean wire to dry in sun.

— *Susan Bingham*

Salmon Loaf

1 large can salmon
1 teaspoon salt
1 teaspoon flour
1 teaspoon cayenne or paprika
1 egg, slightly beaten
1 1/2 teaspoons melted butter
3/4 cup sweet milk
6 teaspoons vinegar

Bone and separate salmon into flakes. Cook all ingredients except the salmon in a double boiler until mixture thickens. Remove from fire and add 1 tablespoon Knox gelatine that has been dissolved in a small amount of cold water. Add salmon after gelatine is thoroughly melted. Turn into mold and chill. Serve in nest of lettuce with dab of mayonnaise topped with dash of paprika as salad, or use sliced for sandwiches.

— *Martha Vance*

Shepherd's Beef Pie

4 cups leftover cooked beef, chopped fine
2 cups leftover gravy
3 cups vegetables, fresh cooked or leftovers
a little chopped onion
seasoning to taste

Cover with mashed potatoes and dot with a little fat. (If you have an egg, beat it and add it to the potatoes before putting over the meat and vegetables.) Bake in hot oven until potatoes are golden brown.

Summer Stew

piece of salt pork about 3 inches square
2 large potatoes cut in small pieces
2 large onions, chopped
4 large ripe tomatoes, skinned

Cover potatoes and onions with water and cook until tender. Dice pork fine and cook until brown but not crisp. Add cooked pork and a little of the drippings to the potatoes and onions. Season to taste, then add chopped tomatoes. Simmer for 20 minutes.

Variation: Use 2 cups corn cut off cob instead of tomatoes, and cook the corn along with the potatoes and onions.

Jerky Gravy

Pound jerky until powdered or flaky. Use a hammer or mallet on an anvil or sadiron to do the pounding.

Put pounded meat into skillet with a little drippings, and stir in some flour. Let it brown to a golden color. Then pour correct amount of milk in slowly, stirring constantly until thick and smooth.

Serve on hot biscuits, potatoes, or other vegetables.

Bean Relish

9 red peppers, seeded
18 green peppers, seeded
11 pieces of celery
18 onions
3 pints vinegar
5 cups sugar
3 tablespoons salt
1 tablespoon mustard seed

Grind first four ingredients. Pour boiling water over them and let stand 10 minutes. Drain. Add vinegar and sugar. Boil 5 minutes and seal when hot.

This is called bean relish because it is good eaten with pinto beans.

— *Della Plumb*

Meat-Stuffed Peppers

8 green peppers
1 small onion, chopped
1 pound ground beef
2 teaspoons fat
4 medium tomatoes, chopped
1 1/2 cups cut fresh corn (3 or 4 ears)
salt and pepper to taste

Remove top and seeds from bell peppers; parboil 5 minutes, drain. Brown onion and meat in hot fat; add tomatoes, corn, and seasonings. Stuff peppers and top with buttered crumbs. Stand upright in greased baking dish. Add small amount of water. Cover and bake in moderate oven at 350 degrees for 1 hour.

— *Lynette Nelson*

Potato Puffs

1 pint mashed potatoes
1 level teaspoon baking powder
1 cup flour
2 eggs
salt

Mix and fry in hot fat.

— *Martha Vance*

Husband Cake

3/4 cup shortening
1 1/2 cups sugar
1 cup tomato juice
3/4 cup water
1 teaspoon soda
3 cups flour
3/4 teaspoon salt
2 teaspoons baking powder
1/2 teaspoon cinnamon
1 teaspoon cloves
1 1/2 teaspoons nutmeg
1 1/2 cups raisins
1 1/2 cups chopped nuts

In a large bowl, cream together shortening and sugar. Combine tomato juice with water; add soda. Add tomato juice mixture and remaining ingredients to creamed mixture and mix well. Bake in a 350 degree oven for 40 minutes. Makes three layers.

— Alice Despain

Pioneer Cookies

1 cup soft butter
1 1/2 cups sugar
2 eggs
1 teaspoon vanilla
4 cups flour

1 teaspoon baking powder
1 teaspoon baking soda
1/2 teaspoon salt
3/4 teaspoon nutmeg
1 cup sour cream

Cream butter and sugar until smooth. Add eggs and beat until fluffy. Stir in vanilla. Sift together flour, baking powder, baking soda, salt and nutmeg. Add sifted ingredients to creamed mixture alternately with sour cream. Chill dough. Roll out on a lightly floured board to 1/4 inch thick and cut in desired shapes. On lightly greased baking tins, bake at 450 degrees for 9 or 10 minutes.

— Gene Christensen

Uncooked Spanish Pickles

1 large cabbage
1 peck green tomatoes
2 red peppers
1 dozen large cucumbers
3 green peppers
1 quart chopped onions
salt
mustard seed
cinnamon and cloves

Chop vegetables, mix and add 1 cup salt. Mix well and let stand overnight. Next day put in jelly bag (flour sack or one of cotton), and press dry. Put 1 gallon water into kettle with 1 ounce of mustard seed. Tie 1 tablespoon cinnamon and 1 tablespoon cloves in a bag. Put on stove and let come to a boil and add vegetables. Return to boil and take off fire. Put in sterilized hot jars and seal.

— Martha Vance

Johnnycake

2 eggs
2 cups buttermilk
2 tablespoons molasses or honey
2 cups cornmeal
1/2 cup flour
1 teaspoon soda
1 teaspoon salt
2 tablespoons fat

Beat eggs until light. Add buttermilk and molasses. Combine with remaining ingredients. Pour in greased dripper and bake in a medium hot oven for about 20 minutes or until done. Makes about 24 large servings.

Vinegar

Pour strained apple juice into dark-colored glass jars, crocks, or watertight wooden containers, leaving 25 per cent headspace to allow for expansion during fermentation. Cover container with something to keep out dust, etc. A triple layer of cheesecloth tied securely with string will do nicely.

Store in cool dark place for 4 to 6 months. After 4 months, test vinegar. If strong enough, strain through triple layer of cheesecloth, pour into bottles, and cork. If too weak, let work a little longer.

For herb vinegar, use fresh herbs and seeds. Drop into vinegar and let sit at least two weeks before using.

— *Diane Wiscles*

Aunt Annie Larson's
Sour Cream Sugar Cookies

1 1/2 cups sugar
1 cup shortening
1 cup thick sour cream
2 eggs, beaten
1 teaspoon lemon or vanilla
5 cups sifted flour
2 teaspoons baking powder
1 teaspoon soda
1/2 teaspoon salt

Cream shortening and sugar well and add beaten eggs. Then add sour cream, stir well, and add extract. Sift flour, soda, and baking powder three times, and then mix all ingredients together. Chill overnight if possible. Roll and cut into any shape. Sprinkle with sugar before baking. Bake in moderate oven till brown.

— *Kathy Webster*

Poverty Cake

(Cake with Filling in the Middle)

2 cups sifted flour	1 cup sugar
2 teaspoons baking powder	2 eggs, well beaten
1/2 teaspoon salt	1 cup milk
1/2 cup shortening	1 teaspoon vanilla

Sift flour, baking powder, and salt together. Cream shortening and sugar until fluffy. Add eggs and beat. Add dry ingredients, milk, and vanilla alternately, beating after each addition. Pour into two 8-inch square pans, putting a little more dough in one pan making a thick layer and then a thin layer. Bake at 350 degrees for 25 minutes. When cool, remove from pans. Cut center out of thick layer, leaving a ring about 1 inch wide on edge. With spatula, split the disc you have removed horizontally, laying half of split disc back in ring. You now have bottom layer prepared for filling.

Filling:

1 quart milk	1 tablespoon flour
4 eggs, well beaten	1 teaspoon vanilla
1 cup sugar	1 tablespoon butter
3 tablespoons corn starch	

Bring milk to boil in a saucepan. Mix eggs, sugar, corn starch, and flour. Slowly add mixture to boiling milk, stirring constantly. Bring mixture to boil again, and cook until moderately thickened. Remove from stove and add 1 teaspoon vanilla and 1 tablespoon butter. Pour into cake shell at once.

Put smaller layer on top. Let cake cool and spread with 2 cups whipped cream, 1/2 cup sugar, and 1 teaspoon vanilla.

— *Lucy Bates*

Grandma Hulsey's

Buttermilk Cookies

2 eggs
2 cups sugar
1 1/2 cups shortening
1 cup buttermilk
1 teaspoon soda
2 teaspoons baking powder
2 teaspoons nutmeg

Add enough flour to above ingredients, to mix stiff enough to roll out and cut with cookie cutter. Bake at 400 degrees for approximately 8 to 10 minutes.

Grandma always took a certain drawstring bag (crocheted and lined) full of these cookies when my mother was a little girl, and they were going on a trip in a wagon with a team called Guy and Hawk. Later, when Mother was eight or ten years old, Grandpa bought a small light wagon for Grandma. They called it a spring wagon because it was lighter and had springs underneath the bed of it that was supposed to make the riding easier. Grandma could hitch up the team as well as any man and drive wherever she needed to go.

— *Myrna Udall*

Plum Pudding

1 cup sugar
1 cup flour
1 1/2 cups bread crumbs
1 cup suet
1 cup milk
1 cup walnuts
1 cup raisins
1/2 teaspoon nutmeg
1/2 teaspoon cinnamon
1/2 teaspoon allspice
1/2 teaspoon cloves
pinch salt
1 teaspoon baking powder

Mix all ingredients. Put into shortening can, filling 3/4 full. Boil 3 1/2 to 4 hours. Serve warm with lemon sauce, or cream with nutmeg and sugar to taste.

— *Lucy Bates*

Vinegar Fizzies

Sift together 2 cups flour, 3 teaspoons baking powder, 1 teaspoon salt. Cut in finely 6 tablespoons shortening. Stir in 2/3 cup milk. Roll and cut into biscuits.

Put 2 cups water, 1 cup vinegar, and 2 cups sugar into baking pan. Heat until sugar is dissolved. Add biscuits to pan, topping each biscuit with a little sugar and butter. Bake in 350 degree oven until golden brown. Serve warm.

— Lucy Bates

Temple Punch

Two ounces citric acid, dissolved in 1 pint boiling water. Ten pounds sugar dissolved in 1 quart hot water. Cool. Four dozen large lemons or enough to make 2 1/2 quarts juice, 3 pints orange juice, 1 quart grapefruit juice, 2 number 2 cans red raspberries, 1 ounce red food coloring. Two pounds bananas optional. Add citric acid and coloring last. Serves 150.

— Martha Vance

Molasses Taffy

2 cups molasses
2 teaspoons vinegar
1 1/2 tablespoons butter or fat
1/8 teaspoon salt
1/2 teaspoon soda

Cook molasses and vinegar in a saucepan slowly, stirring constantly until syrup becomes brittle when tested in cold water.

Remove from fire and add butter or fat, salt, and soda. Stir until mixture ceases to foam. Pour into greased pan. When cool enough to pull, draw the corners toward the center. Remove from pan and pull until light in color and firm. Roll into thin rope or break into pieces. For a different flavor, add a few drops of oil or peppermint before pulling.

Sundown Cobbler

1 cup flour
1 cup sugar
1 cup milk
1 teaspoon baking
   powder
1/2 teaspoon salt
1 egg
1/2 cup melted
   butter
1 quart fruit

Put butter in pan and let it melt in oven. Pour batter into pan after first mixing it in above order. Use fruit or berries, canned or fresh and sweetened. Pour this fruit over the batter. Bake in a 375 degree oven for 30 or 35 minutes.

— *Alice Despain*

Mincemeat

2 pounds meat
2 pounds apples
2 cups seeded raisins
1/4 pound suet, chopped
2 teaspoons salt
1 tablespoon nutmeg
1 tablespoon cinnamon
1 tablespoon cloves
2 cups sugar
1 cup vinegar
1 cup meat liquor

Cook meat and grind. Grind apples. Combine all ingredients and boil gently 2 hours.

— *Lucy Bates*

Hot Water Gingerbread

2 tablespoons shortening
1 1/2 cups sugar
1 egg, well beaten
1 teaspoon soda
1/2 cup molasses
1 1/2 cups flour
1 teaspoon cinnamon
1 teaspoon ginger
3/4 cup boiling water

Mix ingredients in above order. Bake in moderate oven at 350 degrees until done.

— *Alice Despain*

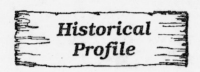

James H. McClintock

(1864-1933)

James H. McClintock will be remembered because he admired the indomitable Mormon pioneers, the "pilgrims of the desert," and wrote the story of their peaceful conquest of Arizona.

McClintock, who was born in Sacramento, came to Arizona Territory in 1879 when he was 15. His career as a cub reporter began at an early age and he worked for newspapers in Prescott, Globe, Tempe, and Phoenix. He was also the Arizona correspondent for the Los Angeles Times.

He rode with Theodore Roosevelt's Rough Riders at San Juan Hill where he was seriously wounded in the leg. He returned to Arizona after his military service and became State Historian in 1919, a post he held for nine years. In 1928 he became postmaster of Phoenix.

The high point of McClintock's life, and that for which he will be remembered, was the publication of his book Mormon Settlement in Arizona: A Record of Peaceful Conquest of the Desert. The book first appeared in 1921 and proved such a valuable addition to Arizona history that the University of Arizona Press reprinted it in 1985. In the reprinted version Charles Peterson notes in the foreword that the Mormon pioneers had been left largely to themselves by serious historians during most of the nineteenth century because "Mormons billed themselves as God's earthly agents; anti-Mormons had presented them as devilish, conspiratorial and degenerate."

McClintock, therefore, exhibited not a little courage in tackling the subject of Mormon pioneers and their influence upon the development and character of the territory. His interest seems to have begun prior to 1916, and the amount of research he did on the subject is evident in his 1921 epic. He portrays the Mormon settlers as heroic figures dedicated to peaceful conquest of the new land. Instead of guns, they brought plows and seeds. They built orchards and fields in the wilderness and grew strong families and community ties. His admiration of these gentle pioneers, "wilderness breakers," as he called them, has stood the test of time.

His research provided much of the information about Mormon pioneer life in Arizona that was used in preparation of this cook book.

About the Author

Daphne Overstreet has been fascinated by the rich heritage of the southwest since she stepped off the train in Tucson over 40 years ago, a young transplant from San Francisco.

On that particular November afternoon, stagecoaches were rambling through downtown streets and "cowboys," "Indians," and a man named Glenn Ford were tethering their horses in front of the old Santa Rita hotel.

Though all the preparations were for a movie, those vivid first memories grew into a deep appreciation for the real history and culture of the area. Through her writings she has tried to preserve a fast fading legacy through meticulous research and interviews with oldtimers.

She has written articles for the *American West Magazine*, *Arizona Highways*, *Desert Magazine*, the *Arizona Republic*, *Tucson Star and Citizen* and the University of Arizona's *Journal of Arizona History*. Her topics include biographical work on Dr. A. E. Douglass, the 1917 Globe copper strike, ghost towns of southern Arizona, Mexican herb lore, territorial cookery, tombstone rubbing and prospecting.

Her book titles include *Festivals of Arizona*, *The Arizona Territory Cook Book 1864-1912*, *Mexico: An Offshore Manufacturing Opportunity* (written at the request of the governors offices of Arizona and Sonora), and *The Offshore Sourcebook*.

Through the years she has also lectured to diverse groups on the topics of her research.

A 1973 honors graduate of the University of Arizona's journalism school, she is a member of Phi Beta Kappa, Phi Kappa Phi and Kappa Tau Alpha honor societies.

Index

Recipe Index

Recipe:_____

From:_____

Ingredients:

_____   _____

_____   _____

_____   _____

_____   _____

_____   _____

Directions:_____

_____

_____

_____

_____

Recipe:_____

From:_____

Ingredients:

_____   _____

_____   _____

_____   _____

_____   _____

_____   _____

Directions:_____

_____

_____

_____

_____

Salsa Lovers Cookbook

More than 180 recipes for salsa, dips, salads, appetizers and more! $9.95

Quick-n-Easy Mexican Recipes

Make your favorite Mexican dishes in record time! Excellent tacos, tostadas, enchiladas and more! $9.95

Chip and Dip Lovers Cookbook

Easy and colorful recipes from Southwestern salsas to quick appetizer dips! $9.95

Tortilla Lovers' Cookbook

Celebrate the tortilla with more than 100 easy recipes for breakfast, lunch, dinner, appetizers and desserts, too! $9.95

Chili Lovers Cookbook

Prize-winning recipes for chili, with or without beans. Plus a variety of taste-tempting foods made with flavorful chile peppers. $9.95

Arizona Cookbook

A collection of more than 350 authentic Arizona recipes. Including Indian, Mexican. and Western foods. $9.95

New Mexico Cookbook

This unique book explores the age-old recipes that are rich with the heritage of New Mexico. $9.95

Easy RV Recipes

Easy recipes for the traveling cook. Over 200 recipes to make in your RV, camper or houseboat. $9.95

Easy Recipes for Wild Game

More than 200 "wild" recipes for large and small game, wild fowl and fish. $9.95

Apple Lovers Cookbook

What's more American than eating apple pie? Try these 150 favorite recipes for appetizers, main and side dishes, muffins, pies, salads, beverages and preserves. $9.95

Pumpkin Lovers Cookbook

More than 175 recipes for soups, breads, muffins, pies, cakes, cheesecakes, cookies and even ice cream! Carving tips, trivia and more. $9.95

Mexican Family Favorites Recipes

250 authentic, homestyle recipes for tacos, tamales, menudo, enchiladas, burros, salsas, frijoles, carne seca, chile rellenos, guacamole, and more! $9.95

ORDER BLANK

GOLDEN WEST PUBLISHERS

☼ 5738 North Central Avenue • Phoenix, AZ 85012

www.goldenwestpublishers.com • 1-800-521-9221 • FAX 602-234-3062

Qty	Title	Price	Amount
	Apple Lovers Cookbook	9.95	
	Arizona Cookbook	9.95	
	Bean Lovers Cookbook	9.95	
	Best Barbecue Recipes	14.95	
	Chili-Lovers' Cookbook	9.95	
	Chip and Dip Lovers Cookbook	9.95	
	Cowboy Cookbook	9.95	
	Easy Recipes for Wild Game	9.95	
	Easy RV Recipes	9.95	
	Grand Canyon Cookbook	9.95	
	Low Fat Mexican Recipes	9.95	
	New Mexico Cookbook	9.95	
	Mexican Family Favorites Cookbook	9.95	
	Peach Lovers Cookbook	9.95	
	Pecan Lovers Cookbook	9.95	
	Quick-n-Easy Mexican Recipes	9.95	
	Salsa Lovers Cookbook	9.95	
	Seafood Lovers Cookbook	9.95	
	Sedona Cookbook	9.95	
	Tequila Cookbook	9.95	
	Texas Cookbook	9.95	
	Tortilla Lovers Cookbook	9.95	
	Veggie Lovers Cookbook	9.95	
	Western Breakfast	9.95	

U.S. Shipping & Handling Add:
(Shipping to all other countries see website.)

1-3 Books $5.00
4+ Books $7.00

Arizona residents add 9.3% sales tax

Total $_____

(Payable in U.S. funds)

☐ My Check or Money Order Enclosed
☐ MasterCard ☐ VISA ☐ Discover ☐ American Express Verification code_____

Acct. No. _____ Exp. Date _____

Signature _____

Name _____ Phone _____

Address _____

City/State/Zip _____

Call for a FREE catalog of all our titles — Prices subject to change —